//Shree Sachchiya Maa/.

Scrum Mantra

The Mantra to Bring Agility at Business Aligning with Industry 4.0

500+ Self-Assessment Quizzical

Mahesh Omprakash Rathi

TM

SCRUM MANTRA

INDIA · SINGAPORE · MALAYSIA

Notion Press

Old No. 38, New No. 6
McNichols Road, Chetpet
Chennai - 600 031

First Published by Notion Press 2019
Copyright © Mahesh Omprakash Rathi 2019
All Rights Reserved.

ISBN 978-1-64678-940-5

Scrum Mantra

Contents

Foreword by Gunther Verheyen

Scrum has been around for 20+ years and has gradually become the most adopted definition of Agile, worldwide. In all modesty, it is unlikely to add or describe viewpoints or descriptions of Scrum, as a whole or in part, that have not yet been articulated somewhere by someone.

Still, there are plenty of important challenges for us, communities of Scrum practitioners. Not just do we face the on-going task of correcting the many misunderstandings that exist over Scrum. We need to continuously look for the best ways and channels to offer to people that want to assess and improve on their understanding of the Scrum framework.

Mahesh, as a distinguished note taker, has compiled all essential information that helped him explore what Scrum has to offer into the book you are now holding, "Scrum Mantra." Mahesh processed his mental and paper notes and created a compendium of highlights and insights to help the reader dig a bit deeper into the Scrum framework.

At the heart, Mahesh conceived his book as an extension of the Scrum Guide. It is designed to help aspiring Scrum practitioners and assessment takers take the next step, to move beyond a literal lecture of the rules and roles of Scrum as stated in the Scrum Guide. It will help the readers take a different look at the problems they face in understanding and expressing Scrum. For this purpose, Mahesh embedded his description in the larger picture of the industrial evolutions, while adding the official guides to more elaborate frameworks such as Evidence-Based Management and Nexus.

All sections have a selection of sample questions to put readers on a path of self-discovery.

– Gunther Verheyen
independent Scrum Caretaker
Antwerp, Belgium

Praise for Scrum Mantra

Scrum has gained popularity over the period of time, not because it is simple in adopting but it is the only framework that enables to think in absolutely an Agile way, and allows one to solve the problems that are intractable, complicated, and complex in nature.

In this book, 'Scrum Mantra – Mantra to bring agility at business aligning with Industry 4.0', Mahesh not only described each and every concept in Scrum, in a very detailed way but also provided readers how the industry is changing every now and then, and why organizations needs Agile coaches in their transformation. This book contains an immense practical value for anyone who is aiming to understand the nuances of, and imbibe the true essence of, Scrum.

Additionally, this book provides many practical scenarios in the form of questions, which is definitely an invaluable asset of knowledge to PSM aspirants, and encourages sharpening their mindset before experiencing the Scrum assessment. This book is a mandatory reader in case you are aspiring to start your Scrum Journey. In this book, Mahesh tried helping people to understand Scrum in a simplest way as well as did a fantastic job of igniting thoughts in Scrum way in form of scenario based questions and left the readers to think on the answers.

This book, in addition to the official Scrum guide, will definitely help the PSM aspirants to achieve success at the assessment as well as at work.

Happy reading and enjoy Scrumming!

Akbar Basha Md, Certified Agile Coach (ICP-ACC), SAFe Agilist, PSM II & PAL

Preface

"Why not write a book to share my notes with all"

I remember during my academic times, many of my friends borrowed my notes for exam preparation. I had developed a habit of writing excellent notes from my school time. After 18 years of time, I have written notes again, now this time on Scrum and Agile for preparing PSM I, PSM II and PAL certification. Whenever I published my certification achievement status on social platform, many of my friends asked me to share my available material for preparing them on these certifications. Hence, the question came in my mind, why not write a book so that everyone can read it and gain the knowledge on Scrum and Agile.

Mantra means "tool of thought" in Sanskrit, a mantra is often used in meditation as a way to harness and focus the mind. My Scrum Mantra is apply Scrum at life. Scrum is simple to understand, and difficult to master. Anyone who applies Scrum at life would definitely thrives, and experience jubilation.

As the father of evolutionary theorem, Charles Darwin, said: "It is not the strongest of the species that survives, nor the most intelligent that survives. It is the one that is the most adaptive to change."

Acknowledgements

A great many thanks to Ken Schwaber and Jeff Sutherland for writing and providing Scrum Guide, which is open for all of us. I have extensively refereed to a vast number of books, blogs and post available on internet

Many thanks to my friend Akbar Basha who reviewed this book and helped me in improving the quality of this book.

My special thanks to all my friends and well-wishers who cannot be named individually, the list being a long one. Their suggestions have helped me and encouraged me in progressing with writing of this book.

This book is dedicated to those who have been with me through years of success and failure.

I would like to acknowledge my father Omprakash Rathi, my mother Meena Rathi, my sister Swati Birla, brother in law Anand Birla, my brother Vijay Rathi and sister in law Kanchan Rathi, for always supporting me.

Thanks to my wife Seema, for managing our home and taking care of our kids when I was busy in writing this book. I really appreciate support from my son Atharv and little girl Ishita who keeps me smiling, they allowed me to write ☺ .

About the Author

Mahesh Rathi is a strong believer in Agile values and principles, and passionate about implementing Agile way across organizations.

Graduated from SRT Marathwada University, with bachelor's degree in the field of Computer Science and Engineering. He is a continuous learner and loves to read books and share the knowledge with the people around. He is one meritorious students from childhood and stood as topper at every stage of his learning. He is always keen at learning new things and adopting them in life and at work.

He is a Certified Professional Agile Leader (PAL) and Professional Scrum Master (PSM) from Scrum.org.

Apart from the academic and professional credentials, he has vast experience in management, leadership areas, efficiently handled billion dollar businesses, which requires collaboration with customers across the globe. He brings with him more than 18 years of rich experience in IT industry. He enabled multiple teams to bring agility at work through leading by example.

Mahesh started his professional career as a software developer and been positioned various roles as, project lead, and project manager elevated to Program manager. He is currently working with worlds top IT Company as a Consultant, helping a group of 200+ associates to enable their Agile journey and making the transformation successful through his impeccable knowledge and expertise.

Mahesh lives in Pune, India with his wife and two kids. He is vivid nature lover and loves to spend his free time with family through trips across different parts of India.

www.scrummantra.com
scrummantra@gmail.com

Chapter 1

Introduction

Evolution of Industry 4.0

Overview

For centuries, most of the goods, including food, clothes, housing, weapons, were manufactured by hand. This changed at the end of the 18th century with the introduction of manufacturing processes, and industrial era Industry 1.0 came to existence. The progress from Industry 1.0 was rapid, and operations rapidly developed from Industry 1.0 to the upcoming Industry 4.0.

Industry 1.0

Industry 1.0 refers to the mechanization of work, which our ancestors used to perform manually, like weaving loom. The late 18th century introduced manufacturing production facilities to the world. Water and steam-powered machines were developed to help workers in the mass production of goods. The first mechanical weaving loom was introduced in 1784.

Industry 2.0

Industry 2.0 was the transformation. The main contributor to this revolution was the development of machines running on electrical energy. The first production line was built in 1870, and the process of mass production was streamlined.

The industry culture introduced in Industry 1.0 was also evolved into the management program to enhance the efficiency of manufacturing facilities. Various production management techniques such as just-in-time manufacturing, lean manufacturing principles, and so on refined the underlying processes leading to improved output.

Industry 3.0

The next industrial revolution was Industry 3.0, where the advent of computers and automation ruled the industrial scene. It was during this period of transformation era where more and more robots were used into the processes to perform the tasks that were performed by humans.

Programmable Logic Controller (PLC) was built in 1969. PLC was a revolutionary invention that signified automation using electronics. The integration of electronics hardware into the manufacturing systems created a requirement of software systems to enable these electronic devices. The entire industry was further automated using electronics and IT.

Industry 4.0

The current industrial revolution is Industry 4.0. Industry 4.0 helps in gathering the data and further integrate it with digital services. The fourth era of the industry is the era of Cyber-Physical Systems (CPS), from 2011. CPS allows the machines to communicate more intelligently with each other without any geographical barriers.

CPS comprises of smart machines, storage systems and production facilities capable of autonomously exchanging information, triggering actions and control each other independently. The Internet of things (IoT) does this exchange of information. In IoT, thousands of sensors work real-time and transfer the data to a local server or a cloud server. The analysis of the available data is carried out by developing predictive models. The study helps the industries improve manufacturing processes, material usage, supply chain, and life cycle management of the product.

The future is now smart technologies like Artificial Intelligence (AI), Data Analytics, Cloud, and so on.

Agile is one of the pillars of Industry 4.0.

Software and Manufacturing

Software Development Vs Manufacturing

Software development and product manufacturing produce products. They include planning, designing, development, testing. Does that mean software development is like manufacturing? The answer is NO. Then what makes the software development and manufacturing different, let us take a look upon it.

In manufacturing, we plan, design, and produce a product and then reproduce it again and again. It is a repetitive process of following the same production sequences.

In software development, we create unique software products entirely. Software is about writing code, logic, and complex algorithms for a particular software product. It is not about replicating the same software product again and again.

Project Management Techniques

Project management techniques in software development are similar to those developed for manufacturing. Manufacturing techniques like Six Sigma, Kanban, Lean, etc. are already adopted in software development.

- Six Sigma is a set of techniques and tools for process improvement. Six Sigma strategies seek to improve the quality of the output of a process by identifying and removing the causes of defects and minimizing variability in manufacturing and business processes.

- Kanban is a scheduling system to improve manufacturing efficiency. Kanban is one method to achieve just in time. It is a strategy for optimizing the flow of stakeholder value through a process that uses a visual, worzk-in-progress limited pull system.

- Lean manufacturing attempts to make obvious what adds value, through reducing everything else if it is not adding value.

Industrial Approach to Software Development

Some of the flaws and misbeliefs of industrial views were:

- Worker staff cannot do important, innovative, and intelligent work.

- The senior team must do critical work. They should plan and design the work for the junior team.

- Senior staff must direct the worker staff with step-by-step instructions.

- Workers can perform only assigned work that is usually repetitive.

- Senior staff must control, review, and track the junior team's work.

The software industry knowingly or unknowingly followed the similar misbeliefs of manufacturing for several years, and some are still following it. Many tried to correct these misbeliefs, for increasing the efficiency of the work, by creating detailed design, upfront planning for the complete software life cycle, assigning responsibility to a particular individual (senior staff), and so on. It did not help at all; in fact, issues and frustration level increased because of applying old industrial methods to software development.

Turning Point in Software Development

Changing the old thinking, mindsets, old way of working, and deep-rooted paradigm is never easy. It took time, in the 1990's many lightweight software development methods evolved. Many software development leaders were following various paths and practices for implementation of the new paradigm. In 2001, a new standard for the software industry was born, formally called 'Agile.'

Agile projects are successful than traditional projects. Scrum is a concrete way to embrace the paradigm of Agile.

Agile

Overview

During the 1990s, several lightweight software development methods evolved. Many software development leaders were following different paths and practices, each being a distinct implementation of the new paradigm. These included:

- Rapid Application Development (RAD), from 1991

- Unified Process (UP) and Dynamic Systems Development Method (DSDM), both from 1994

- Scrum, from 1995

- Crystal Clear and Extreme Programming (XP), both from 1996

- Feature-Driven Development (FDD), from 1997

Although these all originated before the publication of the Agile Manifesto, they are now collectively referred to as Agile Software Development methods.

The official label 'Agile' dates from early 2001, when 17 software development leaders gathered at the Snowbird ski resort in Utah. They discussed their views on lightweight development methods.

Agile was born out of a need to bring efficiency to software development. The gathering resulted in assigning label 'Agile' to the universal principles, beliefs, and thinking of these leaders and their methods. They were published as the 'Manifesto for Agile Software Development.'

Definition of Agile

Agile means able to move quickly and easily. Agile is the ability to respond to change. Agile is a set of values and principles. Agile is a collection of beliefs that team can use for making decisions about how to do the work of building a product.

Agile software development is more than frameworks such as Scrum, Extreme Programming, or Feature-Driven Development (FDD). Agile software development is more than practices such as pair programming, stand-ups, and Sprints.

Agile software development is an umbrella term for a set of frameworks and practices based on the values and principles expressed in the Manifesto for Agile Software Development and the 12 Principles behind it.

Agile software development is a methodology to build the product or provide the service incrementally using short iterations. In Agile software development, requirements and solutions evolve through the collaborative effort of self-organizing and cross-functional teams and their customers/end users.

- Agility is the state of high responsiveness, speed, and adaptiveness while controlling risks.

- Agility is about mindset; it is about behavior; it is about cultural change.

- Agile is driven by the continuous collaboration of people ranging over all required departments whether they are called business, IT, marketing, sales, operations, or management. People are respected for their creativity, intelligence, and self-organizing capabilities.

- Agile replaces the traditional command-and-control mechanism of assigning individuals on a daily basis with executable micro-tasks.

- Agile teams are facilitated by servant-leadership. Boundaries and a context for self-management exist, upon which teams are given objectives and direction. Subtle control emerges from the boundaries.

- Agile makes it explicit that success and progress in software development can only be determined by frequently inspecting working software and the actual value, it holds for the people who will have to use it. High-value needs are addressed first.

- New insights, evolving opinions, and changed priorities form the heart of Agile. Agile encourages change as a source of innovation and improvement. As unanticipated things will happen, a learning perspective is needed to adopt the Agile.

- Every Agile process slices time into time-boxed iterations, periods having a fixed start and end date. This time management technique focuses on delivering value and ensures regular checks so that lessons learned can be incorporated from one iteration to the next.

- Agile requires a different organizational structure. The Agile organization is a growing, learning, adapting, living organism rather than a steady-state machine that follows an existing business model.

Manifesto

Based on 17 software development leader's combined experience of developing software and helping others do that, the seventeen signatories to the manifesto for Agile Software Development proclaimed that they value (Beck et al., 2001):

- Individuals and Interactions over processes and tools

- Working Software over comprehensive documentation

- Customer Collaboration over contract negotiation

- Responding to Change over following a plan

That is to say, the items on the left are valued more than the items on the right.

- Tools and processes are important, but it is more important to have competent people working together effectively.

- Good documentation is useful in helping people to understand how the software is built and how to use it, but the main point of development is to create software, not documentation.

- A contract is important but is no substitute for working closely with customers to discover what they need.

- A project plan is important, but it must not be too rigid to accommodate changes in technology or the environment, stakeholders' priorities, and people's understanding of the problem and its solution.

Principles behind Agile Manifesto

The Manifesto for Agile Software Development is based on twelve principles (Beck et al., 2001):

1. Our highest priority is to satisfy the customer through early and continuous delivery of valuable software.

2. Welcome changing requirements, even late in development. Agile processes harness change for the customer's competitive advantage.

3. Deliver working software frequently, from a couple of weeks to a couple of months, with a preference to the shorter timescale.

4. Business people and developers must work together daily throughout the project.

5. Build projects around motivated individuals. Give them the environment and support they need, and trust them to get the job done.

6. The most efficient and effective method of conveying information to and within a Development Team is face-to-face conversation.

7. Working software is the primary measure of progress.

8. Agile processes promote sustainable development. The sponsors, developers, and users should be able to maintain a constant pace indefinitely.

9. Continuous attention to technical excellence and good design enhances agility.

10. Simplicity - the art of maximizing the amount of work not done is essential.

11. The best architectures, requirements, and designs emerge from self-organizing teams.

12. At regular intervals, the team reflects on how to become more effective, then tunes and adjusts its behavior accordingly.

Advantages and disadvantages of Agile

Some of the advantages of Agile:

- Fast results - The potentially shippable Product Increment is delivered in each iteration.

- Improved return on investment – In shorter iterations, potentially shippable Product Increment of the highest possible value is delivered. Features are provided incrementally; hence, benefits are realized early while the product is in the development process.

- Higher customer satisfaction & delighted customers. A business person works together (often in the same room) with the Development Team. The progress of development has high visibility, ability to adapt to changing requirements, and continuous delivery of Product Increment implies high engagement and customer satisfaction.

- High product quality. Testing is done in each iteration. Early feedback from customers allows improving product quality.

- Reduced risk. Early delivery of business value in each iteration lowers the risk associated with development.

- Reduced costs.

- Reduce the chances of complete product failure as the customer can see the Product Increment starting from the first iteration. The controlled risk to one or a couple of iterations (release).

- Optimize the predictability.

- Employee satisfaction.

- Confidence to succeed in a complex world.

- More joy.

Some of the disadvantages of Agile:

- Sometimes it may be challenging to set the final delivery date, as you keep on adding new features and new Sprints at any time. In complex projects, at the beginning itself, it is difficult to calculate the accurate efforts required.

- If customer participation is lacking or the customer is not clear on the outcome he or she wants, it may affect the project results.

- Documentation can be neglected. Agile teams should find the right balance between documentation and discussion.

Waterfall vs Agile

The Waterfall model was the first Software Development Life Cycle (SDLC) Model used widely in Software Development. The Waterfall model is a breakdown of project activities into linear sequential phases, where each phase depends on the deliverables of the previous one and corresponds to a specialization of tasks. It is also called as a linear-sequential life cycle model. The output of one phase acts as the input for the next phase sequentially.

Waterfall Model:

Waterfall development enables performing the task according to the organization's specialized departments. A schedule is defined with deadlines, and a product proceeds through the various phases of the development.

Development moves from concept, requirement, design, implementation, testing, deployment, installation, troubleshooting, and ends up at operation and maintenance. Each phase of development proceeds in the defined order.

Some of the advantages of the Waterfall Model:

- The model is simple and easy to understand.

- Easy to manage, one phase is completed at a time before starting the next phase.

- Comprehensive documentation is done. All requirements are captured in detail in the requirement phase.

- A comprehensive plan is developed upfront; all milestones are defined and understood by everyone.

- Process and results are well documented.

Disadvantages of Waterfall Model:

- No working software is produced until late during the life cycle.

- Critical learning occurs after the major analyze-design-code-test loop.

- Scope changes later in the project once requirement phase is completed are not welcomed.

- High amounts of risk and uncertainty if requirements are not clear or fixed at the beginning of the life cycle.

- Return on investment is late, after completing all phases and the complete product is deployed.

Transformation from Waterfall to Agile

Are you finding it difficult to make changes during development, using the Waterfall model? This is what a team usually encounters when they use the Waterfall model for project development.

Agile methods are better than the Waterfall because of the following reasons:

- Being flexible - Waterfall methodology leaves no space for sudden changes or modifications; the changes required may not be that easy to implement. On the other hand, Agile methods are not that rigid and have ample room for flexibility. Flexibility is one of the strongest advantages of the Agile model.

- Moving towards customer satisfaction - Waterfall model as per its basic structure does not focus on the client. It is more focused on helping the internal team sail through the successful execution of the project. This leaves no room for the involvement of the client during a project. Agile is more focused on customer satisfaction. This allows the participation of the customers even during the development phases, thus enabling them to give their inputs and observations during the development of the project.

- Testing along with development phase - In the Waterfall model, the testing phase comes in place only after the build phase has been completed. After having completed four out of the six steps of the model, you can start with the testing phase. Although it may suit some projects, on the more significant parts, it affects the projects. In Agile, the testing can happen in concurrence with the project development phase, thereby making things easier for the project Development Team.

- Early return on investment - Other reasons that make Agile methods counter better than the Waterfall models is the possibility of an early return on investment along with better quality and alignment in the development process. Moreover, you can build the right products and get real-time feedback from your customers.

Plan driven project management needs to be replaced with Agile way of working.

Table 1: Waterfall way Vs Agile way

Waterfall way	Agile way
The entire plan is created upfront and work is done as per fixed plan	Planning is done iteratively, and work is done iteratively
Development is phase-based	Development is iterative
Each decision is made in its proper phase – Ex. design is finalized in the design phase	Decision steps are made iteratively – Ex. design emerge across multiple iterations
Testing is done after a build phase	Testing is done in the same iteration as development

Waterfall way	Agile way
Critical learning occurs after a significant analyze-design-code-test loop	Learning occurs continuously through multiple iterations
Time, budget and scope traded off for one another	Time and budget are held constant, scope varies
Complete planning is done at the beginning of the project	The plan is revised continuously over time and becomes more accurate
Scope changes later in the project are not welcomed	Scope changes later in the project are welcomed
Process centric - Ex. Fulfilling assignments on time	Value centric - Ex. Delivering potentially shippable Product Increment

Agile vs Lean

The lean movement was born in Japan in the mid-1950-s in the manufacturing industry and was mainly aimed at loss reduction and sustainable production. Lean is a set of principles that educate, motivate, coach, and value people to continuously optimize their work and how they work. People can use these principles to create better products faster yet sustainably and respectfully. People do their best with the means and tools they are given in their actual situation.

The lean process should be designed upon its principles and thinking and be constantly tuned to the actual situation. There is not any definite predefined Lean process with prescribed phases, roles, definitions, artifacts, deliverables, etc.

Lean manufacturing attempts to make obvious what adds value, through reducing everything else because it is not adding value. Lean manufacturing is a systematic method for the minimization of waste within a manufacturing system without sacrificing productivity.

In the 2000s, Lean was also adapted for software development by Mary and Tom Poppendiecks, who related it with seven initial Lean principles and Agile philosophy.

The seven principles of Lean development are:

1. Eliminate Waste

2. Build Quality In

3. Create Knowledge

4. Defer Commitment (not to plan in excessive detail for months in advance)

5. Deliver Fast

6. Respect People

7. Optimize the Whole

The most popular Lean development tools are Pair programming, Test-driven development, Minimize wait states, Automation, Code reviews, Documentation, Knowledge sharing sessions, Training, etc.

A typical lean company follows a learn-measure-build cycle, and conducts many tests, frequently connects with customers, understands their value and focuses its key processes to improve continuously. A never-ending cycle leads the organization to sustainability, smart development, and success.

Lean Process Mapping (Value Stream Mapping):

Also known as Value Stream Mapping, lean process mapping is described as a lean tool that uses a flow diagram to document each step of the process. Many lean professionals view value stream mapping as a vital tool for identifying waste, reducing process cycle times, and improving processes. A Value Stream Map is a visual tool used to see ways to enhance the flow of the product. It demonstrates how information flows and demonstrates information gaps to help the product. It coordinates to improve efforts continually. Toyota Motor Company developed the initial Value Stream Mapping model and enforced it via material and process flow diagrams. This Value Stream Mapping demonstrated the essential process steps that existed from order entry to final shipment of the product and helped obtain a broad perspective of the activities of the company. It enabled Toyota to eliminate non-essential waste-creating operations while preserving the production process.

Similarities and differences between Agile and Lean methodologies:

Most teams practicing Lean and Agile do not have a clear understanding of the similarities or the differences between these two methodologies. In the simplest way: Agile development is a process for rapid software delivery that is connected to many Lean principles. There are more than just a few similarities between Agile and Lean. Lean and Agile are truly blended philosophies. Agile has distinct practices that match the main Lean principles very well.

Strategies and concepts in Agile that are rooted in Lean Principles are:

- Iterative Development: Iterative development aligns with the Lean principles of Deliver Fast and Defer Commitment. Lean encourages teams to deliver fast by managing flow - limiting the amount of work-in-process (WIP) to reduce context switching and improve focus. The Lean principle of Defer Commitment says that Lean organizations should function as just-in-time systems, waiting until the last responsible moment to make decisions. This allows Lean organizations to have the agility to make informed decisions, with the most relevant, up-to-date information available.

- Short Feedback Loops: Lean thinking encourages this definition of waste: If a customer would not pay for it, it is waste. Short feedback loops between Agile developers and their stakeholders' help teams create a habit of eliminating processes, activities, and products that do not directly result in customer value.

- Disciplined Project Management Process - Frequent review and adaption: A disciplined process allows teams to practice the Lean principle of Build Quality In. The concept is simple; Automate and standardize any tedious, repeatable process, or any process that is prone to human error. This principle allows Lean teams to error-proof significant portions of their processes, so they can focus their energy on creating value for their customers. Relying on a consistent, disciplined process allows Agile teams to refine and optimize their processes for value delivery continuously.

Verheyen Gunther has listed the consistency in principles of Lean and Agile as following (Gunther, 2019).

Table 2: The consistency in principles of Agile and Lean

Agile	Lean
Self-organizing teams	Respect for People
Inspect & adapt, short feedback cycles	Kaizen
No unused specs, architecture or infrastructure	Prevent/eliminate waste
Estimates reflect team capacity	Pull inventory
Information radiators	Visual Management
Definition of Done, Engineering standards	Built-in Quality
Active Business Collaboration	Customer Value
Whole Team Together	Optimizing the whole
Time-boxed iterations with working increments	Deliver Faster
The facilitating servant-leader	The manager-teacher

Now let us see some differences between Agile and Lean (www.miro.com, 2019).

Table 3: Differences between Agile and Lean

Agile Philosophy	Lean Philosophy
Is aimed at executing tasks faster, adapting to changes easier	Is about smart development, by eliminating anything that doesn't bring value to the customer
Makes the developing process flexible	Makes the developing process sustainable
Was initially designed for Software Development, then expanded to Marketing, and is currently applied in other areas	Started from traditional manufacturing and expanded to all existing industries
Action loop: Product Backlog - Sprint Backlog - iteration (Sprints) - potentially shippable result	Action loop: build-measure-learn
Method for demonstrating progress - Definition of Done	Method for demonstrating progress - validated learning
Methodologies: Scrum, XP, FDD, DSDM, Crystal Methods, etc.	Methodologies: Kanban, Kaizen ,etc.
Toolkit: Sprints, boards, Scrum Master, acceptance tests, user story mapping etc.	Toolkit: hypotheses, customer interviews, funnel and cohort analysis, Customer Success Manager, etc.

Kanban vs Scrum

Kanban uses Lean concepts such as limiting work in progress to improve results. Kanban is a visual workflow management method that enables organizations with the visibility, metrics, and focuses they need to manage work and people in a better way.

Kanban is a strategy for optimizing the flow of stakeholder value through a process that uses a visual, work-in-progress limited pull system. Visualize work increase communication and collaboration. Central to the definition of Kanban is the concept of "flow." Flow is the movement of customer value throughout the product development system. Kanban optimizes flow by improving the overall efficiency, effectiveness, and predictability of a process. Kanban limits the amount of work in progress to reduce context switching and improve focus.

Similarities between Scrum and Kanban:

They track processes via the scheduling system to ensure transparency, and they are managed by devoted teams. Both methodologies limit the amount of work in progress (Scrum limits them by time units — iterations, Kanban limits work in progress per workflow state). In addition, Scrum and Kanban focus teams on breaking the work into pieces and supplying the releasable parts of the product earlier and more often.

Despite these similarities, Scrum and Kanban are not the same, and the table 4 illustrates some of the differences. (www.miro.com, 2019).

Table 4: Differences between Scrum and Kanban

Scrum	Kanban
Time-boxed interactions prescribed	Time-boxed interactions optional
Cross-functional teams prescribed	Cross-functional teams optional, specialist team allowed
Items broken down so they can be completed within one Sprint	No particular item size is prescribed
WIP limited indirectly (per Sprint)	WIP limited directly (per workflow state)
Prescribes three roles	Doesn't prescribe any roles
A Scrum board is reset between each Sprint	A Kanban board is persistent
Prescribes a prioritized Product Backlog	Prioritization is optional

How to decide when to use Kanban and when to use Scrum:

Scrum and Kanban are not competitors or enemies. Both are a means to help teams and their stakeholders achieve sustainable success. Following are conditions under which Kanban is a better fit than Scrum:

- Low Tolerance for Change: Scrum needs a revolutionary and transformative change, starting from Scrum roles, meetings, etc. Kanban does not use transformative change; it embraces evolutionary change. Kanban employs a start with what you do now mindset that introduces teams to the shallow end of the pool before taking them toward the deep end of maturity. Kanban does not require any changes to roles or meetings when first getting started.

- Obvious at All Levels: The primary advantage Kanban has over Scrum is that it is immediately intuitive to anyone. A Kanban board is an instant sense-making device. It requires zero explanation to understand. However, Kanban's primary advantage is also its biggest flaw. It is easy to be fooled by Kanban's hidden sophistication. Kanban is far more sophisticated than a simple tool for visualization. Kanban is built for speed, but most teams will never master the behaviors that produce those results because their commitment to learning Kanban stops at visualization.

- Fluid Priorities: Scrum produces the best results when a team commits to a batch of work and is empowered to remain focused for the duration of its iteration. Kanban encourages optionality. A Kanban team prefers to not commit to working in batches, and they do not commit to work until they start it. This means a Kanban team can be maximally flexible in responding to emergencies or changing priorities without needing to renegotiate commitments.

- Complex Collaboration: If your team has a large number of activities, the strategies of Sprinting ahead or using a scaling framework may introduce unnecessary complexity and delay. Kanban does not utilize time-boxing to create predictability; it uses lead-time—so it is capable of sustainably supporting an unlimited number of activities and collaborations.

DevOps

DevOps and continuous delivery have always been part of Scrum. In order to deploy to production faster and deliver higher quality value to customers, Scrum and DevOps engineering practices must integrate. DevOps is the union of people, processes, and products to enable continuous delivery of value to end-users.

DevOps is a process to develop, deliver, and operate software. DevOps promotes collaboration between Development and Operations team to deploy code to production faster, in an automated & repeatable way. In simple words, DevOps can be defined as the alignment of development and IT operations with better communication and collaboration.

DevOps is a software development approach that includes Continuous Development, Continuous Testing, Continuous Integration, Continuous Deployment, and Continuous Monitoring of the software throughout its development life cycle. Agile Scrum, Lean, Six Sigma DMAIC, etc. can serve as efficient enablers for DevOps. However, DevOps is not meant to be seen as an improved and combined superset of these methodologies and techniques.

With DevOps, your self-organized teams can deliver potentially shippable Product Increments every day. In many organizations, I have seen many teams following a lot of processes and checklist before releasing code on the production system. Teams used to send downtime email to all the users of the product so that they can complete the deployment. Some teams used to do the deployments on weekends or by staying late in the office. DevOps allows you to release your code many times a day at any time without affecting your end-users of the product.

Continuous Delivery, CI and CD

- Continuous Delivery - Continuous Delivery aims at building, testing, and releasing software with higher speed and frequency.

Continuous delivery is a software engineering approach in which teams produce software in short cycles, ensuring that the software can be reliably released at any time. It releases the software manually (not through automated deployments).

• The approach helps reduce the cost, time, and risk of delivering changes by allowing for more incremental updates to applications in production. A straightforward and repeatable deployment process is essential for continuous delivery. Continuous delivery aims to keep the code in a deployable state at any given time. This does not mean the code or project is 100% complete, but the available feature sets are tested, debugged, and ready to deploy, although you may not deploy at that moment.

• Continuous Deployment (CD) - Continuous Deployment, a similar approach in which software is also produced in short cycles but through automated deployments rather than manual ones. Automation will help the team to increase its speed and frequency of delivery. With Continuous Deployment, every change that is made is automatically deployed to production. Continuous Deployment requires continuous delivery. The difference is between deployment methods (Manual Vs Automated).

• Continuous Integration (CI) - Continuous Integration is merging all code from all developers to one central branch many times a day trying to avoid conflicts in the code in the future. The concept here is to have multiple developers on a project to keep the main branch of the repository to the most current form of the source code, so each developer can check out or pull from the latest code to avoid conflicts.

Continuous Delivery and DevOps

Continuous Delivery and DevOps are similar in their meanings and are often conflated, but they are two different concepts. DevOps has a broader scope, and centers on the cultural change, specifically the collaboration of the various teams involved in software delivery (developers, operations, quality assurance, management, etc.), as well as automating the processes in software delivery. Continuous Delivery, on the other hand, is an approach to automate the delivery aspect and focuses on bringing together different processes and executing them more quickly and more frequently. Thus, DevOps can be a product of Continuous Delivery, and Continuous Delivery flows directly into DevOps.

Scaling Frameworks

Scrum teams are small. The scaling model is necessary for multiple teams working on large complex projects. The key success criteria that must be attained before scaling is to ensure that Agile works well with one to six teams and ensure that these teams release software to production at the end of each Sprint while increasing their velocity and value to their customers at each iteration.

Some of scaling frameworks are:

- SAFe (Scaled Agile Framework)

- LeSS (Large Scale Scrum)

- Nexus

SAFe

Scaled Agile Framework (SAFe) allows enterprises to accomplish their organizational goals to produce the highest quality product in the shortest sustainable amount of time. An approach scales Scrum to an Enterprise Level and gives you the freedom to scale according to your business needs. It introduces a philosophy of servant and lean-Agile leadership and goes beyond just implementing an organizational structure, rather instills a new mindset. SAFe can be easily extended and scaled to hundreds or even thousands of team members.

Organization Structure:

You need to change your existing organizational structure to adopt SAFe. It is not an overnight process. It take its time. There are guides available on the Scaled Agile Framework's website that gives a systematic insight into transitioning to SAFe.

Some of the features of SAFe are:

- Designed for large enterprises, makes it easier to work with multiple teams.

- Well defined organizational structure, with designated roles and responsibilities.

- Lean processes that mean there is a minimal waste, thus ensuring that the teams focus on what really needs to be done.

- The formation of the Agile Release Train helps to maintain collaboration amongst teams. The Agile Release Train (ART) is the primary value delivery construct in SAFe. The Agile Release Train is a long-lived, self-organizing team of Agile teams. Each team is a virtual organization (5 to 12 teams) that plans, commits, and executes together. Agile Release Trains align teams to a common business and technology mission.

- Very well documented which is available for consultation.

- Comprehensive and innovative approach as the teams relentlessly improves and adopt newer ways of working.

- Limits the Work in Process (WIP) to keep the teams more focused to produce a higher quality of work.

- Elaborate handling of processes from the team level to the high level.

- Promotes trust, collaboration, and transparency between the development and the top management.

- Emphasizes on attaining business value in the shortest sustainable time.

- Ensures consistent approach towards planning, execution, and delivery.

- Promotes the sharing of strategy, common vision, and architecture amongst the development and the managerial teams.

- Constant feedback from customers helps maintain a successful business relationship leaving room for improvement throughout the entire process.

LeSS

Large Scale Scrum (LeSS) is one of the leading frameworks of Agile software development. It is a multi-team Scrum framework applied to an Agile team consisting of twelve, hundreds or even thousands of individuals, working together on one specific shared product.

Using LeSS, you can create large or small-sized products. It is a simple and minimalistic framework where there is less enforcement of rules, processes, roles, or artifacts. There are only conventional Scrum roles such as the Product Owner, Scrum Master, and the team.

LeSS is very customer-centric as teams get to interact directly with the customer while the Product Owner focuses on setting the roadmap, priorities, and the long-term vision of the product.

There are two types of LeSS:

- Basic LeSS is for 2 to 8 teams

- LeSS Huge is for more than 8 teams

Organization Structure:

You may need to abandon your current organizational structure and change your present development techniques drastically to embrace LeSS completely. The organizational structure is completely different from traditional program management. It is recommended by LeSS to start applying principles of LeSS with one Scrum team and adapt the change systematically.

Some of the features of LeSS are:

- LeSS provides the complete product view, which guarantees transparency in the work you do.

- The teams are in direct contact with the customer that enables the teams to grasp the real idea of what the customer needs.

- With lean thinking, there is minimal waste, thus ensuring focus on what needs to be done.

- There is ample room for the team to learn and grow consistently.

- Teams are feature-oriented and customer-centric.

- Dependencies are handled at the integration level by sharing the code base with other teams. More frequent code integration is recommended to avoid complexities.

- The role of management is focused on defining the vision and nurturing of the team members. Product Owner defines and prioritizes the high-level requirements for the teams.

- Teams coordinate with each other frequently and share the codebase.

- There are design and architecture workshops to align synergy across all the teams and focus towards the end product.

- Frequent Retrospectives and inspect and adapt sessions help ensure continuous improvement.

- Heavily focused on the Product Owner.

- No guidelines on portfolio management.

- Items are in Basic LeSS while epics exist in LeSS Huge.

- The role of the Scrum Master fades away once the teams become proficient in LeSS.

Nexus

Nexus is a simple framework that implements Scrum at scale across multiple teams to deliver a single integrated product. Teams work in a common development environment and are focused on producing a combined Increment every Sprint with minimal dependencies. It can be applied to 3–9 Scrum teams. So cannot be scaled to more than nine teams and not more than a hundred practitioners.

Organization Structure:

No change in existing organizational structure is needed. It can be adopted in your current organization; all you need is knowledge of Scrum.

Features:

- This framework promotes and ensures transparency, continuous integration, and relentless improvement.

- Having a single product and Sprint Backlog boasts transparency as all the teams Sprint data can be easily visualized. Daily Scrums enhance communication and help erase dependencies.

- Working in a shared environment where work is continuously being integrated into one.

- The final product guarantees continuous integration.

- Teams use automation to manage any complexities.

- The Nexus Integration teams give the necessary support and facilitation to the teams in order to keep them in line. Thus eliminating the need for Scrum of Scrums meeting that is an essential part of other scaling frameworks. They make sure, if the processes are followed and truly work as servant leaders to ensure that the teams flourish.

- The teams confirm relentless improvement with activities like the refinement of the Product Backlog, Sprint Review, and Sprint Retrospective.

- Listening to feedback from the stakeholders is paramount. It is vital to adapt to any changing requirements and to eliminate any waste with Lean-Thinking.

Sample Questions

Note: All type of questions are present in this book - Multiple choice questions, True or False, Yes or No, select one, select all applicable. If anything is not mentioned explicitly about how many options you need to select, default is only one. Answers are not shared in this book, as I want you to study and find your own answers. Visit website scrummantra. com for more questions and verifying your answers.

Q: One developer Winston asked Agile coach Ozzy that what is the primary benefit of an Agile approach compared to a Waterfall. What should Ozzy answer?

1. Deliver with reduced risks
2. Deliver on-time, on-budget, and on-scope
3. Deliver the potentially shippable valuable Product Increment as soon as possible, in accordance with the correct quality level
4. All of the above
5. None of the above

Q: Alice, one senior developer said, an Agile strategy has an advantage in making projects less complex by planning and implementing in smaller increments. Do you agree with Alice? Yes or No

Q: A newly joined Agile coach Jay asked Senior Agile coach Sandra, if you have to select one Agile objective, what will you select?

1. Deliver with reduced risks
2. Deliver on-time, on-budget, and on-scope
3. Improvement of customer satisfaction
4. Utilization of people increases
5. Efficiency of the deliverable increases

Q: David, an Agile coach asked team member Angelina to select true statement from the following. What should Angelina select?

1. Agile is for scaling while Scrum is for small teams
2. Agile is one of an execution way of Scrum

3. Scrum is an implementation of Agile Development

4. Agile and Scrum are alternative terms for the same methodology

Q: As per Agile, delivering the potentially shippable valuable Product Increment is the most important and documentation is a waste of time. True or False

Q: What will Agile coach Franka, infer from a sustainable pace?

1. Team member should not change their velocity else team will not achieve sustainable pace

2. Keep on working for longer duration to complete the delivery as long as you are getting extra compensation.

3. The team should establish a velocity that can be sustained within normal hours of operation

4. Working as many number of hours as needed to deliver the potentially shippable valuable Product Increment

Q: The major benefit of an Agile development is to increase the capability of a team to deliver on time, on budget, and on-scope. True or False

Q: Read the Agile Manifesto and select the correct statement

1. There are 12 core values of the Agile Manifesto

2. People are more essential than contracts

3. Working shippable software is important and documentation is a waste of time

4. Planning is not needed in Agile, always respond to customer by accepting the change requests

Q: Your colleague Marion wants to know what is common in all Agile approaches. Select the best option.

1. A fixed iteration length

2. Iterative development and incremental delivery

3. An emphasis on on-time delivery as per schedule

4. Deliver with reduced risks

Q: A team is working on an Agile project from last two months. Two new change requests (CR) are arrived while iteration is running. What should team do?

1. Agile means accepting changes at any time. Hence, CRs are considered in the current work of the iteration.

2. Not considered in the current iteration and excluded until next iteration.

3. CRs are evaluated for importance. If it is more valuable to the business, included in the iteration and some of the less priority requirements are pushed back to the Backlog list.

4. Added in the Backlog list so that all stakeholders can considered after the project is completed.

Chapter 2

Scrum

Overview

Scrum is an Agile approach for developing products and services. It is a replacement for traditional plan driven model. The complete cultural and organizational mindset change is needed to achieve the Agility. A shift is required from the traditional way of working to one that embraces a culture of self-organization and collaboration.

Scrum approach is appropriate for not only work with uncertain requirements or frequent changes in requirements but also when technologies are uncertain. Scrum is neither a methodology nor a recipe book solution to the organization's problems.

Scrum enables one to visualize the dysfunctions and waste that prevent the organization from reaching their true potential (Kenneth S. Rubin, Essential Scrum).

Hirotaka Takeuchi and Ikujiro Nonaka introduced the term "Scrum" in the context of product development in their 1986 Harvard Business Review article, "The New New Product Development Game." They related teams to Scrum formations in Rugby, as one cross-functional team performs the whole process across multiple overlapping phases, in which the team "tries to go the distance as a unit, passing the ball back and forth." In rugby football, a Scrum is used to restart play, as the forwards of each team interlock with their heads down and attempt to gain possession of the ball.

In 1995, Sutherland and Schwaber jointly presented a paper describing the Scrum framework at the Business Object Design and Implementation Workshop held as part of Object-Oriented Programming, Systems, Languages & Applications '95 (OOPSLA

'95) in Austin, Texas. Over the following years, Schwaber and Sutherland collaborated to combine this material—with their experience and evolving good practice—to develop what became known as Scrum.

In 2001, Jeff and Ken were amongst the 17 software development leaders creating the Manifesto for Agile Software Development at a Snowbird ski resort in Utah.

In 2002, Ken Schwaber founded the Scrum Alliance with Mike Cohn and Esther Derby. Ken chaired the organization. Certified Scrum accreditation series was created and launched.

In 2006, Jeff Sutherland created his own company, Scrum.inc. He continues to offer and teach the Certified Scrum courses through Scrum Alliance.

In late 2009, Schwaber left the Scrum Alliance and founded Scrum. org which oversees the parallel Professional Scrum accreditation series.

In 2010, a public document called The Scrum Guide had officially defined Scrum. It has been revised 5 times, with the current version being November 2017.

Definition of Scrum

Scrum is a framework for developing, delivering, and sustaining complex products incrementally. Scrum is based on empiricism that addresses the unpredictability of complex product development. Scrum emphasizes the teamwork and all team members are equally accountable. Scrum embraces an iterative and incremental approach to deliver a working product.

Scrum is a framework within which people can address complex adaptive problems, while productively and creatively delivering products of the highest possible value.

Scrum is

- Lightweight

- Simple to understand

- Difficult to master

Scrum is a process framework that has been used to manage work on complex products since the early 1990s. Scrum is not a process, technique, or definitive method. Instead, it is a framework within which you can employ various processes and techniques. Scrum makes clear the relative efficacy of your product management and work techniques so that you can continuously improve the product, the team, and the working environment

The Scrum framework consists of Scrum Teams and their associated roles, events, artifacts, and rules. Each component within the framework serves a specific purpose and is essential to Scrum's success and usage.

The rules of Scrum bind together the roles, events, and artifacts, governing the relationships and interaction between them. All its parts are needed in order to be effective. Scrum's role, artifacts, events, and rules are fixed and cannot be changed based on different implementation. That means they are immutable. If they are changed then the implementation is not called Scrum.

Uses of Scrum

Scrum was initially developed for managing and developing products. Starting in the early 1990s, Scrum has been used extensively, worldwide, to:

1. Research and identify viable markets, technologies, and product capabilities

2. Develop products and enhancements

3. Release products and enhancements, as frequently as many times per day

4. Develop and sustain Cloud (online, secure, on-demand) and other operational environments for product use

5. Sustain and renew products.

Scrum has been used to develop software, hardware, embedded software, networks of interacting function, autonomous vehicles, schools, government, marketing, managing the operation of organizations and almost everything we use in our daily lives, as individuals and societies.

As technology, market, and environmental complexities and their interactions have rapidly increased, Scrum's utility in dealing with complexity is proven daily.

Scrum proved especially useful in iterative and incremental knowledge transfer. Scrum is now widely used for products, services, and the management of the parent organization.

The essence of Scrum is a small team of people. The individual team is highly flexible and adaptive. These strengths continue operating in single, several, many, and networks of teams that develop, release, operate and sustain the work and work products of thousands of people. They collaborate and interoperate through sophisticated development architectures and target release environments.

Scrum Benefits

- Delighted customers
- Employee satisfaction
- Improved return on investment (ROI)
- Reduced costs

- Fast results

- Confidence to succeed in a complex world

Scrum at a Glance

Let us see the Scrum at a glance. A list of the things that the system should include and address like functionality, features, technology, and so on is called Product Backlog. The Product Backlog is an ordered list of all product requirements. Items that are on top of the Product Backlog are the ones that are the most desired. Product Backlog content can come from users, customers, sales, marketing, engineering, and so on. Only the Product Owner (PO) can decide the order of the Backlog and decides the order in which things are built.

Small, cross-functional team perform all development. This team is called the Development Team (DT). Development Team takes on as much Product Backlog Items as they think they can turn into an Increment of product functionality within a fixed duration iteration, which is called Sprint. Sprint's duration typically takes one to four weeks. Every Sprint must finish by delivering new executable product functionality, a potential shippable Product Increment.

Scrum relies on team initiative and integrity. During the Sprint, a servant leader called as Scrum Master (SM) enforces Scrum practices and help the Development Team to make decisions.

A Product Owner, Development Team, and Scrum Master collectively called a Scrum Team.

The Scrum Teams and within which Development Teams are self-organizing and fully self-directed. It means that members of the Development Team are capable to do their work and no one outside the Development Team manage their work. Teams that are self-organized select best way to do their job. Self-organization has and requires boundaries, boundaries within which self-organization happens. The

Development Team decides on how to turn the Product Backlog Items into a Product Increment.

Every Sprint begins with Sprint Planning. Scrum team performs Sprint Planning to determine the most important subset of Product Backlog Items to build. The Development Team maintains a list of selected Product Backlog Items and tasks to perform during each Sprint that is called a Sprint Backlog. Sprint Backlog solely belongs to the Development Team.

The Development Team meets daily to inspect and adapt its progress, called the Daily Scrum. At the Daily Scrum, impediments are identified for removal.

At the end of the Sprint, the Scrum Team gets together with all stakeholders at a Sprint Review meeting to inspect the Product Increment. The thirty-day Sprint duration ensures that the worst that happens is that thirty days are lost should the team prove unable to develop any useful product functionality. At the end of every Sprint, the Product Owner decides whether or not to fund the next Sprint.

Scrum team reviews the process used to develop the Product Increment, called Sprint Retrospective. Scrum Team identifies improvements to be implemented in the next Sprint.

The team then goes through another iteration of work, and the next Sprint starts immediately after completion of Sprint Retrospective.

Sample Questions

Q: A Multi-National Company WashLeh was following Waterfall model for several decades. A new CEO Brian was appointed and company has decided to be Agile in next one year and will be adopting Scrum. Few seniors suggested modifying the Scrum terminology to make it similar to the current situation. Select all applicable.

1. The change from Waterfall to Scrum may not be apparent to everyone as old terminology has deep roots, hence some benefits may be missing.
2. As Scrum is a framework, it can be adopted in this way.
3. Scrum is not prescriptive; hence, organization can get good results by doing these modifications.
4. Organization may feel less excited about the change from Waterfall to Scrum adoption.

Q: A team was believing that the main reason for adopting the Scrum is it reduces cost as Scrum teams work more proficiently and deliver more value in a smaller amount time. True or False

Q: A newly joined Scrum Master, Jennifer thinks some parts of Scrum can be implemented without implementing the complete Scrum model. Do you agree with Jennifer? Yes or No

Q: A newly joined developer, Atharv asks a question to the Scrum Team - What does it imply to be cross-functional for a Development Team?

1. Development team comprises of developers and a sub team of functional expertize. Collectively it is called as cross-functional team.
2. Development Team members work closely with external specialist like developers, and testers who are not part of the team.

3. The Development Team comprises of developers and specialist like architects, and testers.

4. The Development Team consist of individuals that have all necessary skillsets collectively to deliver the Product Increment.

Q: One developer, Aarya was telling another newly joined developer Donald that the Scrum is a lightweight framework that includes guidelines for documentation. Do you agree with Aarya? Yes or No

Q: A junior developer Debra feels Face to face, communication is the best way of communication; teams must be co-located to use Scrum. Do you agree with Debra? True or False

Q: The working culture of a Scrum is a hierarchical structure of Development Team. True or False

Q: A developer Aanvi said core of the Scrum is the Scrum Guide. Do you agree with Aanvi. Yes or No

Q: Essence of the Scrum is the Sprints of short duration. True or False

Q: Essence of the Scrum is a small team of individuals, which is highly flexible and adaptive. True or False

Q: Heart of the Scrum is the Development Team that delivered potentially shippable product. True or False

Q: Moritiz asked his friend Gael where could he use Scrum? Help yourself in selecting Gael's answer from following. Select all applicable.

1. Sustain and renew products
2. Development of products and enhancements
3. Research and identifying of viable markets, technologies, and product capabilities
4. Development of software and hardware
5. Manage the organization's operations

Q: A developer Fabian said as per his understanding of Scrum Guide, Scrum advises using only those Scrum elements and rules that are appropriate for a specific project. Do you agree with Fabian? Yes or No

Q: In a group discussion on Scrum in a startup organization, a debate was going on and few said Scrum is not a process or technique. What is your opinion on this? True or False

Q: What is Scrum?

1. An enhanced Waterfall framework derived from Agile methodology to address complex adaptive problems while delivering potentially shippable valuable products.
2. A framework within which people can address complex adaptive problems while delivering potentially shippable valuable products.
3. It is a simple software development methodology for delivering potentially shippable valuable products.
4. It is a simple software development technology for delivering potentially shippable valuable products.

Q: What kind of documentation is found in Scrum projects? Select the best.

1. Updated User Manual at the end of each iteration
2. All type of documentation done using Jira
3. Just enough documentation for planning, to support the development, and use of the product. And it will be supplemented by further face-to-face discussions
4. to support the development and use of the product
5. Documentation is a waste of time, Scrum suggests face-to-face conversation

Q: Yukta, a junior developer said Scrum is a container for a set of methodologies, processes and techniques. Is this true? Yes or No

Q: What are the correct statements? Select all applicable

1. Scrum is only for startups for developing and maintaining complex products
2. Scrum is developed to remove Waterfall from the market
3. Scrum is a framework for developing and maintaining complex products
4. Scrum is based on empirical process control theory

Q: Scrum is a software development methodology. True or False

Q: Scrum is a Process Framework. True or False

Q: Which of the following does not describe Scrum? Select all applicable

1. Simple to understand
2. A software development process
3. Difficult to master
4. A method for developing and maintaining complex products
5. A lightweight framework

Q: The Scrum approach for documentation is. Select the best

1. Documentation is a waste of time
2. Just enough documentation to support the development
3. Do enough documentation that can be used during appraisal discussion
4. Documentation is more important than writing the code

Q: A developer Swati with 10 years of software development experience however new to Agile believes that Scrum is a methodology for developing and maintaining complex products. Do you agree with Swati? True or False

Q: In a Scrum Project, the team should strive for a sustainable pace and normal working hours in a week. True or False

Q: At the beginning of the iteration, there is less work and the team works longer hours towards the end of the iteration. True or False

Q: One of the reason organizations started adopting Agile and Scrum is they wanted to remain up to date with the latest trend in the market. True or False

Q: In a Scrum Team, less experienced team members are allocated the simpler tasks.

Q: As there is only one role as developer in Development Team, Scrum team ensures blame is allocated equally. True or False

Q: Which are the incorrect statements about the Scrum? Select all applicable

1. A methodology to develop software.
2. Scrum is not based on empirical process control theory.
3. A recipe book that defines best practices, rules, and procedures for software development.
4. A defined prescriptive, iterative and incremental process.

Chapter 3

Scrum Theory

Overview

Scrum is founded on empirical process control theory or empiricism. Empiricism asserts that knowledge comes from experience and making decisions based on what is known. Scrum employs an iterative, incremental approach to optimize predictability and control risk.

Empiricism is a theory that states that knowledge comes primarily from observation, practical experience, and experiments.

Traditional processes (also known as open-loop systems or forward) are replaced in Scrum with the empiricism of closed-loop systems.

An open-loop system is a system without feedback. In an open-loop system, subsystems are created to control complex problems. The output of the previous subsystem becomes the input to the next subsystem. In situations of unpredictable changes, deviations and variances accumulate across various subsystems and get detected only at the end of the final subsystem.

A closed-loop system is a system with feedback. In a closed-loop system (in contrast to an open-loop system), the actual result of the system is regularly inspected with the desired result to improve the quality. This creates transparency. Most appropriate adaption is done to close the gap between actual and desired outputs.

Scrum implements regular inspection and adaption opportunities. Two specific closed-loop feedback cycles are the 24-hour cycle The Daily Scrum and the container The Sprint.

Three pillars that uphold every implementation of empirical process control are Transparency, Inspection, and Adaptation.

Transparency

Significant aspects of the process must be visible to those responsible for the outcome. Transparency requires those aspects to be defined by a common standard, so observers share a common understanding of what is being seen.

For example:

- All participants must share a common language referring to the process.

- Those performing the work and those inspecting the resulting Increment must share a common definition of Done.

Inspection

Scrum users must frequently inspect Scrum artifacts and progress toward a Sprint Goal to detect undesirable variances. Their inspection should not be so frequent that inspection gets in the way of the work. Inspections are most beneficial when diligently performed by skilled inspectors at the point of work.

Adaptation

If an inspector determines that one or more aspects of a process deviate outside acceptable limits and the resulting product will be unacceptable, then the process or the material being processed must be adjusted. An adjustment must be made as soon as possible to minimize further deviation.

Scrum prescribes four formal events for inspection and adaptation, as described in the Scrum Events section.

- Sprint Planning

- Daily Scrum

- Sprint Review

- Sprint Retrospective

Self-Organization

Scrum Teams are self-organized. Self-organization means the team decides how to do the work, while the business decides what to develop. Any decisions related to the work should be left to the self-organizing team. Self-organization means organizing and managing yourself, not needing control by any external authority. Self-organization happens, and it cannot be forced on the Scrum team. Self-organization is not about limitless freedom, and it happens within the boundaries (Ex. Scrum rules like time box, the Definition of Done to be met). Self-organizing teams reduce their dependency on management and increase their ownership of the work; however, management should remove obstacles that are preventing Scrum team to self-organize.

The Development Team collaborates to deliver the potentially shippable valuable Product Increment. The Development Team members believe in the success of the team is more important than the success of the individual. Organization rewarding outstanding individual performer to only a few top-performers.

A Scrum team should not be built by adding any random individuals to the team. If we just put seven random individuals together, then we should not expect good results to come. Those who are responsible for initiating the Scrum project should select the individuals carefully to comprise the Scrum team.

Workspace

It is essential to equip a team with adequate tools and infrastructure. Use open working environments that allow people to communicate more efficiently, make it easier to get together, and facilitate self-organization. Flexible work area and infrastructure encourage creative culture.

Scrum Team's workspace is the environments that are space-efficient, productive, and vibrant. The team shares the workspace for their daily work. In a good Scrum workspace, there is plenty of open space to move around in, there is lots of open wall space for planning and task boards, desks are configured for conversation, and telephone & network are distributed throughout. The worktables should be modular and movable to allow the teams to configure, as they desire to optimize communication and collaboration.

The wide, open setting means high visibility. It can ease communication if you know someone is sitting at his or her desk, and you can just walk over. The shared workspace helps the team in making the decisions quickly.

The most efficient and effective method of conveying information to and within a Development Team is a face-to-face conversation (co-location is best but not mandatory). A Scrum team always requires a shared workspace even if they are working from different location and they can achieve this using modern communication technologies. A distributed team with modern communication facilities will be as dynamic as a co-located team.

Scrum at Life

Scrum, a framework that is not only used for software development but can also be used and applied at life, to bring in a lot of joy, value and a constant focus towards achieving set goals and keeping up the priorities.

Anyone who applies Scrum at life would definitely thrive, and experience jubilation. If we look at the three pillars of Scrum from a different perspective, they also play a vital role in sustaining the lifestyle. At any point in time, it is good and necessary to constantly look upon and work on these three elements (pillars) in order to have a remarkable journey towards an amazing and promising life.

We must be true (TRANSPARENT) to ourselves, our family/ friends, and the people around us. It generates faith in ourselves, the individuals around us and sends the positive vibes across. Many of the times, transparency avoids disputes among the individuals (either at work or at home), and it shows our righteousness in a way, and we get trusted; and, obviously strengthens the relations with people.

Whatever situation may we come across (be it good or bad), one thing which is must to do is INSPECTing, our pathways, actions, and behavior; it helps in correcting, achieving and augmenting our goals (again, be it personal or professional). An inspection does not go in vain when we profoundly look for ways to improvise. Definitely, one can always find different ways to improve and inspire through regular inspections. A sincere inspection of what are we doing now and what more can we do much better, impulses our future prospects.

We are living in a VUCA (Volatile, Uncertain, Complex and Ambiguous) world, things will not/never always be as we anticipate, we should neither stick to the way we ought to be nor inflexible, rather we must ADAPT and realize the fact that change is constant and evolves, and may also move quickly from one facet to other. The adaptation nature in oneself, not only develops resilience but also encourages in facing the challenges, and, cheering up even when fails, as one will intrinsically start taking the failures as learning/feedback.

To experience a vivid and versatile life, apply Scrum at work and at life.

Sample Questions

Q: In a Pune based startup organization, a project was started using Scrum. Sprint duration was two-week. Three Sprint completed successfully. In fourth Sprint, only two days are left for Sprint closure. Development Team was confused about one of the PBIs and asked Product Owner Kyary for two extra days to finish that PBI work. What do you think Kyary should do?

1. Kyary asks the Development Team to stick to the committed Product Backlog Items.
2. She asks the Development Team to stick to the two-week Sprint time-box.
3. She raises concern to the Scrum Master and ask SM to teach Development Team on stick to the two-week Sprint.
4. She extends the Sprint duration and inform Development Team that she will not extend it again.
5. Both 3 & 4

Q: A new developer was asking on the meaning of self-organization in a Scrum team. What are you going to say about what a self-organized team can handle? Select all applicable.

1. Managing their work to achieve a common goal
2. Doing the appraisal reviews of each other, hence no need of managers
3. Firing low performing team members as self-organization means no need of HR and managers for handling this activity
4. Always open to support and manage other teams which are developing other products and are from the same organization

Q: The Development Team is self-organized, and Self-organization is more effective when it happens within boundaries. Scrum framework provides the boundaries for self-organization. Select two.

1. Creating a potentially shippable product Increment by the end of each Sprint
2. Time-boxing all events that limit the possibility of going off-track
3. All Development Team members should have all skillsets and should have equal domain knowledge
4. Always open to support and manage other teams which are developing other products and are from the same organization

Q: Self-organization means the team decides how to do the work, while the business decides what to develop. True of False

Q: One of the developer Jennifer found that one or more elements of a process differ from acceptable boundaries. She was confused whether to wait for some time as sometimes things gets resolved automatically over the period. What do you think when correction is needed?

1. Waiting is a good option to get it resolved automatically
2. First discuss deviations with HR and get all the details clarified
3. Wait till Daily Scrum and then discuss with other developers at the Daily Scrum, and then an adjustment can be made
4. To minimize any more deviations as quickly as possible

Q: Scrum Master Cameron was teaching about Scrum framework. Abby, the developer asked her one question on the frequency of inspection. Ryuhei, another developer answered this question as – inspection is important, however if the frequency of inspection is very high, then it can interfere with the Development Team's job. Do you agree with Ryuhei? Yes or No

Q: Scrum Master was taking one session on Scrum. Scrum Master shared following list and asked about the most essential items out of this list in any Scrum project. What do you think? List – A) Time-boxing of events B) Self-organization, C) Working overtime, D) Detailed documentation, E) Continuous improvement

1. A, B, C, D
2. A, B, C
3. A, B,D
4. B, E
5. A, B, E
6. A, B, D, E

Q: Two developers were arguing on the fact that Scrum employs an iterative and incremental approach so that management can control the Development Team in planning and estimating in the agreed iteration length. Do you agree? Yes or No

Q: Natalie found that one or more elements of a process differ from acceptable boundaries. She decided not do anything and added these deviations as a Product Backlog Items in Product Backlog. Did she perform the right thing? True or False

Q: Can you select pillars that uphold Scrum? Select all applicable

1. Transparency
2. Flexibility
3. Creativity
4. Inspection
5. Productivity
6. Adaptation
7. Agility

Q: Can you help in finding out the type of process control Scrum is based on?

1. Non Waterfall
2. Historical
3. Self-organization
4. Empirical

Q: Scrum employs incremental and iterative approach to maximize investment returns and increase visibility. True or False

Q: What are the benefits of iterative and incremental approach?

1. Monitoring is easy in small iterations and Product Increment is easy to verify
2. Improved ROI
3. Optimize predictability
4. All of the above
5. Both 2 and 3

Q: Scrum employs an iterative and incremental approach to make sure there is transparency in the resource utilization that optimize the processes and people. True or False

Q: Empiricism asserts that knowledge comes from experience and making decisions based on what is known. Can you select what does empiricism provides? Select all applicable

1. More occasions to discuss many possibilities, hence uncertainty can be eliminated
2. More occasions to discuss many possibilities
3. More occasions to make informed decisions and reducing risk
4. More occasions to spend time on non-project activities

Q: In Scrum, transparency means the process should be more visible to management and less visible to Development Team members as developers focus more on the Product Increment. True or False

Q: Anand said transparency is best described as whole process should be visible to everyone. Do you agree with Anand? Yes or No

Q: If I ask you to describe transparency, how would you best describe it?

1. The whole process must be visible to key stakeholders.
2. The whole process must be visible to everyone.

3. Significant aspects of the process must be visible to those responsible for the outcome.

4. All of the above.

Q: A new startup company in Pune, India was discussing that Scrum is only useful for software development projects. However, Mamie the developer says, Scrum can be used for support and maintenance related work. Do you agree with Mamie? Yes or No

Q: How would you best describe on doing early design in Scrum projects?

1. Every Sprint is equivalent to a project in a Waterfall model. Hence, design must be done after requirement analysis phase is done in the Sprint.

2. Sprint is not same as Waterfall project, hence there is no design in Scrum project.

3. 70% design should be done upfront, 30% as needed.

4. Just enough design upfront should be done to start with and it helps to mitigate risk.

Q: Scrum increases the opportunity to control risk and optimizes the predictability of progress. True or False.

Q: Scrum uses the new terminology for the same traditional practices and processes; hence, everyone is adopting Scrum and Agile.

Q: Scrum is suitable for complex problems as well because of the following. Select all applicable

1. It is easier to master in comparison with the traditional way

2. It is closely associated with digital technologies

3. Scrum is developed for Industry 4.0

4. None of the above

Chapter 4

Scrum Values

The framework of Scrum is based upon following core values:

- Commitment
- Courage
- Focus
- Openness
- Respect

Scrum Values are the backbone for a Scrum Team's processes, practices, activities, interactions, and behavior. These values are centered on people and the way they self-organize and work collaboratively.

When the values of commitment, courage, focus, openness and respect are embodied and lived by the Scrum Team, the Scrum pillars of transparency, inspection, and adaptation come to life and build trust for everyone. Lack of trust affects commitment, courage, focus, openness and respect in the Scrum Team. The Scrum Team members learn and explore those values as they work with the Scrum roles, events, and artifacts.

Successful use of Scrum depends on people becoming more proficient in living these five values.

- People personally *"commit"* to achieving the goals of the Scrum Team.
- The Scrum Team members have *"courage"* to do the right thing and work on tough problems.

- Everyone *"focuses"* on the work of the Sprint and the goals of the Scrum Team.

- The Scrum Team and its stakeholders agree to be *"open"* about all the work and the challenges with performing the work.

- Scrum Team members *"respect"* each other to be capable, independent people.

Commitment

Commitment is the dedication, devotion, responsibility, or the obligation of people to achieve the goals of the Scrum Team.

A general definition of commitment is the state or quality of being dedicated to a cause, activity, etc. Commitment is about dedication and applies to the actions and the intensity of the effort. In Scrum, Commitment is not about the final result.

The Scrum team members commit to themselves, to the team, to the organization.

The Scrum Team commits to

- Agile values and principles

- The Sprint Goal

- Collaborate & self-organize

- Excellence & perform the best they can

- Empiricism

- Continuous improve

- Finish the work

- Deliver potentially shippable Product Increment

Few myths about 'commitment' are:

- All requirements selected in the Sprint must be completed by the end of the Sprint.

- The expectation of the Scrum framework that the team should predict, commit, and achieve the final Sprint results like a contract.

Few examples:

- I always understand what the Sprint Goal is and do everything possible to finish my work to achieve the goal.

- I keep myself available for the events and always reach on time. I know the Definition of Done and what all needs to be done to say that a Product Backlog Item is Done.

Courage

Members of the Scrum Team have the courage to do the right thing and work on hard issues. They have the courage to share risks, share all information transparently, and ask for help if stuck in any task.

The Scrum Team shows courage in responding to change over following a fixed plan. They show courage in forecasting the Product Backlog Items that are challenging to estimate, courage in doing the right estimation even if estimation increases from earlier estimation. Courage to inform incomplete Product Backlog Items and not to deliver partially completed items.

It takes courage to share a different opinion with a team member and engage in productive conflict.

- The Scrum Team members show courage in not building stuff that nobody wants.

- They show courage in accepting people for who they are.

- Scrum Team shows courage to acknowledge their mistakes.

- They show courage by taking any difficult decisions.

Few examples:

- If I see something that is wrong with what I am being asked to do, I will say so.

- I question my team members if I feel that they are doing something wrong.

- I stand firm if I believe I am right, even if I am in the minority within the group.

Focus

Everyone is focused on the Sprint's work and Scrum Team's goals.

- Scrum Team members focus on the work committed to do, focus on what is most important now, and focus on making it happen.

- Daily Scrum helps people to focus on daily work.

- Scrum Team focuses on the Product Backlog Items which are in progress and important to be completed, instead of working on all Product Backlog Items and not completing any before Sprint expires.

- Scrum Team members focus on work as a team and collaborate.

- They focus on delivering potentially shippable Increment.

Few examples:

- If I complete the current task, I will take the next item that is the most important task to the team even if it is not my preferred task as per my specialty.

- Even if I hate documentation, I would be a professional and help team with documentation. So that items will move from in progress to done before Sprint expiry.

- I always give attention to user stories irrespective of enjoying or not enjoying working on it

Openness

The Scrum Team and its stakeholders agree to be open about all the work and the challenges with performing the work.

- Scrum Team members are open to collaborate and help others in the team and in the organization.

- They are open to learning from one another.

- Scrum Teams are open to change and try new things.

- They are transparent about their work and sharing the feedback.

- Openness enables team members to share their perspectives, feel heard by their peers, and be able to support team decisions

Few examples:

- In the Sprint Review, the Development Team openly shows what they did, and stakeholders openly give feedback.

- In Sprint Retrospective, Scrum Team members are open to change and accept new ideas.

- I openly tell any hard news to team members.

- I openly give feedback to others and receive the feedback openly from others.

Respect

Scrum Team members respect each other to be capable and independent people.

- Scrum Team members show respect for people.

- They respect each other with their strengths and weakness.

- They respect everyone's opinions.

- They know customers change the requirements, and they show respect for customers by responding to changes.

- They respect the Scrum roles.

- When everyone's opinions and perspectives are respected, we can say with absolute certainty that everyone has the chance to be heard.

Few examples:

- The Development Team gives each other feedback in an honest and respectful manner.

- I respect everyone's opinion and listen when others are talking.

- I trust that everyone works and communicates with good intentions.

- I feel that my opinion is respected and I value everyone's opinion equally.

- I respect an individual's background.

- I feel I have been heard and I support team decisions even if the decision was not my preference.

Sample Questions

Q: A Scrum team of 7 members is working on a banking project. They are following two week Sprint. Mark is a manager for the embedded software group, he requires the Development Team member Seema (as she earlier worked on the similar type of software tools used in the embedded group) to support a critical work which is essential for their company. Scrum Team completed one week of the Sprint. Mark approached Seema for supporting that critical task. What is recommended for Seema to do?

1. Seema should ask Mark to speak to Scrum Master
2. Seema should ask Mark to speak to Product Owner
3. Seema should support Mark as she worked in an embedded group in the past and they both belongs to one company
4. Seema should say 'No' to Mark's request respectfully and explain Mark about her responsibility for the Scrum Team

Q: Scrum is a framework for delivering products of the highest possible value. Which Scrum values are displayed if Product Backlog Items with low business value are not constructed?

1. Commitment & Courage
2. Focus & Openness
3. Respect
4. Commitment, courage, focus, openness, and respect
5. Transparency & Focus

Q: A Scrum project is started with 6 developers and with two-week Sprints. 4 Sprints are completed. Keira, a Development Team member complains at the Retrospective that no one listens to her suggestions. She said it is happening continuously in the complete Sprint. Which Scrum values are affected here? Select three

1. Commitment
2. Courage
3. Focus
4. Spirit
5. Respect
6. Openness

Q: Angelina and Swapnil are two important stakeholders for a Scrum project with two weeks Sprint. Fifth Sprint was started and on fourth day, Angelina asked Mike a Development Team member to help her with an urgent task. Task was not a part of the goal for the Sprint. Mike was not sure about what to do. Angelina informed him that Swapnil also want Mike to work on this task. Mike started working on that task for complete day and successfully finished it. He has not informed about working on this task to the Product Owner. You have to select one correct statement from the following.

1. Mike should have checked with Swapnil before implementing the task
2. Mike should have consulted with his supervisor before implementing the task
3. Mike did the correct thing as both Angelina and Swapnil are important stakeholders and Scrum also suggest Development Team should be open for changes.
4. Mike did not display the Scrum value of focus.

Q: Can you select the correct statements about the Scrum team from following?

1. Changes are expected and welcomed by the Scrum team
2. Courage to adapt
3. Development Team has only three roles
4. All of these

5. Both 1 & 2

6. Both 1 & 3

Q: Two developers Claudio and Akshay were not trusting each other since last Sprint because of some miscommunication between them. Scrum Master Margot observed this and decided to teach Development Team on the Scrum values that are impacted when there is a lack of trust in the Scrum team. Can you select which are those Scrum values?

1. Commitment & Courage

2. Openness & Transparency

3. Focus & Openness

4. Trust & Respect

5. Respect

6. Commitment, Courage, Focus, Openness, and Respect.

Chapter 5

Scrum Framework

Overview

Scrum framework consists of 11 elements - three Roles, three Artifacts, and five Events. They are good enough, minimal but sufficient.

Roles

Scrum organizes its players into Scrum Teams. A Scrum team consists of three roles, where each role complements the other roles in accountability.

- A Product Owner

- A Development Team

- A Scrum Master

The Product Owner is a one-person role who ensures that the right solution is developed. PO acts as a voice of stakeholders (internal and external), customers, and users. Product Owner decides what to build, the order in which is to build and communicates the same to the Development Team.

The Development Team consists of professionals who do the work of delivering a potentially releasable Increment of Done product at the end of each Sprint.

The Scrum Master is a one-person role. Scrum Master is a knowledgeable person about the Scrum. The Scrum Master is responsible for promoting and supporting Scrum. Scrum Masters do this by helping everyone understand the Scrum theory, practices, rules, and values. The Scrum Master is a servant-leader for the Scrum Team. The Scrum Master acts as a coach to both the Development Team and the Product Owner.

Artifacts

Scrum artifacts increases transparency of crucial information so that everyone has the same understanding of the artifact.

There are three Scrum Artifacts:

- Product Backlog
- Sprint Backlog
- Product Increment

Product Backlog is an ordered list of product requirements. It is a single source of requirements and is accessible to the Scrum team and all stakeholders. As long as the product exists, Product Backlog exists.

Sprint Backlog is a list of the Product Backlog Items pulled into a Sprint and an associated plan (expressed in terms of tasks that are estimated in ideal hours) to get the Product Backlog Items Done. Sprint Backlog is an artifact created at a Sprint Planning meeting and updated continuously during Sprint execution.

Product Increment is a piece of working software that adds previously created increments and as a whole form a software product.

Events

Scrum has five formal events.

- The Sprint

- Sprint Planning

- Daily Scrum

- Sprint Review

- Sprint Retrospective

These prescribed events are used in Scrum to create regularity and minimize the need for meetings not defined in Scrum. All events are time-boxed events, which means every event has a maximum duration. The events may end once the purpose of the event is achieved. The Sprint is a heart of Scrum, and this event is a container of all other events. Once a Sprint begins, its duration is fixed and cannot be shortened or lengthened. It can be canceled before Sprint-box is over.

All events are the opportunities to inspect and adapt something.

Sprint Planning, Daily Scrum, Sprint Review, and Sprint Retrospective events are the formal opportunities to inspect and adapt while the container event Sprint presents several informal opportunities to inspect and adapt. Events are specially designed to enable transparency and inspection. Failure to include any of these events results in reduced transparency and is a lost opportunity to inspect and adapt. Let us take a very brief look at the events mentioned above.

Sprint Planning is an event that kick starts each Sprint and is where the Scrum team discusses which Product Backlog Items will be included in Sprint. The time-box of this meeting is 8 hours for monthly Sprint. For shorter Sprints, the event is usually shorter.

Daily Scrum is an opportunity for the Development Team to assess progress towards achieving the Sprint Goal and plan their activities for the next 24 hours. Time-box of this event is strictly 15 minutes.

Sprint Review usually takes place on the last day of the Sprint and provides the team an opportunity to show the Done Increment to stakeholders. The time-box for this event is 4 hours for a monthly Sprint. For shorter Sprints, the event is usually shorter.

Sprint Retrospective is the final meeting in the Sprint. This is the event in which Scrum team reviews what could be improved for future Sprints from the process viewpoint, and how should they do it. The time-box of this event is 3 hours for monthly Sprint. For shorter Sprints, the event is usually shorter.

Scrum allows additional meetings (that are not defined in Scrum) if they facilitate achieving the Sprint Goal.

Product Backlog Refinement is the act of adding detail, estimates, and order to items in the Product Backlog. This is not a formal event of Scrum.

Sample Questions

Q: The products developed using Scrum approach will be cheaper than those developed using by any other approach. True or False.

Q: The products developed using Scrum approach will be more costly than those developed using other approach. However, they will be of top quality as their reviews are done in every Sprint. True or False.

Q: Scrum does not allow extra meetings that are not listed in Scrum. All events prescribed by Scrum are sufficient to inspect and adapt. Do you agree? Yes or No

Q: One of the advantage of the Scrum framework is that it increases team's ability to deliver on-time, on-budget, and on-scope. True or False.

Q: What comprises Scrum? Select four

1. Values
2. Artifacts
3. Transparency
4. Rules
5. Events
6. Roles

Q: Check all the formal opportunities to inspect and adapt

1. The Sprint Planning
2. The Daily Scrum
3. The Sprint Review
4. The Sprint Retrospective
5. The Sprint

Q: The Scrum Master can be a part of the Development Team and Product Owner cannot. True or False

Q: Could the Product Owner be a part of the Development Team? Yes or No

Q: Could the Scrum Master be a part of the Development Team? Yes or No

Q: Can you select main events defined in Scrum Framework from following? A) Sprint Planning, B) Sprint Retrospective, C) Sprint Review, D) Quality Review, E) Daily Scrum

1. A, B, C, D, E
2. A, B, C, D
3. A, B, C, E
4. A, C, D, E

Q: What does the Scrum Framework mainly define?

1. Rules & Roles
2. Document guidelines
3. Artifacts and events
4. Quality guidelines
5. Both 1 & 3
6. Both 2 & 3

Q: Scrum Master Olivia in a Scrum session was explaining that every event in Scrum has a time-box. Can you explain me on what does 'time-box' means here?

1. The event must start at defined start time
2. The event must end at defined end time and cannot end before or after that
3. The event must complete within a predefined time limit
4. All of the above
5. None of the above

Q: Scrum's artifacts, events, roles, and rules are immutable. True or False?

Q: Can you select all applicable statements about a Scrum Framework?

1. Encourages Scrum team to meet frequently
2. Only one additional meeting is allowed apart from regular Scrum events so time should be spent on the developing Product Increment
3. Scrum Master should be supervisor for all developers as Scrum recommends one developer cannot be supervisor of other one
4. Product Owner is the supervisor of Scrum Master
5. All of the above
6. None of the above

Chapter 6

Scrum Team

The Scrum Team consists of three roles:

- A Product Owner
- The Development Team
- A Scrum Master

Each role complements the other roles in accountability, thereby tuning collaboration into the key to success.

- The Scrum Master serves the Development Team and the Product Owner.
- The Development Team serves the Product Owner.
- The Product Owner serves the stakeholders.

Scrum Teams are self-organizing and cross-functional. Self-organizing teams choose how best to accomplish their work, rather than being directed by others outside the team.

Cross-functional teams have all competencies needed to accomplish the work without depending on others not part of the team. As cross-functional teams do not spend time waiting for individuals outside the team to do the work, team members have an excellent chance to deliver a Done Increment that gives value to users. Cross-functional teams promote team members to get things done outside their comfort zone. They have more possibilities to develop their skills by learning from other.

The team model in Scrum is designed to optimize flexibility, creativity, and productivity. The Scrum Team has proven itself to be increasingly effective for all the earlier stated uses, and any complex work.

Scrum Teams deliver products iteratively and incrementally, maximizing opportunities for feedback. Incremental deliveries of Done product ensure a potentially useful version of working product is always available.

The Product Owner

Overview

The Product Owner is responsible for maximizing the value of the product resulting from the work of the Development Team. How this is done may vary widely across organizations, Scrum Teams, and individuals.

The Product Owner is the sole person responsible for managing the Product Backlog.

Product Backlog management includes:

- Clearly expressing Product Backlog Items

- Ordering the items in the Product Backlog to best achieve goals and missions

- Optimizing the value of the work the Development Team performs

- Ensuring that the Product Backlog is visible, transparent, and clear to all, and shows what the Scrum Team will work on next

- Ensuring the Development Team understands items in the Product Backlog to the level needed

The Product Owner may do the above work, or have the Development Team do it. However, the Product Owner remains accountable.

One product has only one Product Backlog and only one Product Owner (There is one Product Owner for more than one Scrum team working on the same Product Backlog). The Product Owner is one person (a single person might be both a Product Owner and a team member on the same Scrum team), not a committee. The Product Owner may represent the desires of a committee in the Product Backlog, but those wanting to change a Product Backlog item's priority must address the Product Owner.

The Product Owner decides on releasing the Product Increment to the market. The Product Owner tracks total work remaining at least every Sprint Review; he or she projects likely target and delivery dates based on progress to date.

For the Product Owner to succeed, the entire organization must respect his or her decisions. The Product Owner's decisions are visible in the content and ordering of the Product Backlog. No one can force the Development Team to work from a different set of requirements, and the Development Team is not allowed to act on what anyone else says.

Product Owner encourages the Development Team to work directly with the stakeholders and users for clarification on a PBI so that he or she does not become a bottleneck.

The Product Owner ensures a PBI is detailed only when it seems sure it is likely to be implemented; it minimize waste in developing and sustaining the Product Backlog.

Only the Product Owner has the authority to cancel a Sprint, although he or she may do so under influence from the stakeholders, the Development Team, or the Scrum Master.

Key Responsibilities

Product Owners key responsibilities are:

- The Product Owner works with the Development team to establish a Sprint Goal. The Product Owner is responsible for monitoring the progress towards the project goal and maximize the value of the product.

- Product Owner gives inputs to the Development Team to select a set of Product Backlog Items.

- Ultimately, the Product Owner is accountable for ensuring that the grooming activities are carried out. The Product Owner, may not write all of the Product Backlog Items on her own; others may help to write it down.

- Product Owner is responsible for sharing her bandwidth and being available for questions and clarification whenever Development Team has any.

- Product Owner is responsible for defining the acceptance criteria for Product Backlog Items. Development Team or might contribute for writing and executing the acceptance tests, however the Product Owner is accountable.

- The Product Owner takes the decision on ROI by deciding on appropriate scope, duration, and budget. The Product Owner decides whether to fund the next Sprint.

The Development Team

Overview

In Software development industry, it is very common to see roles such as programmer, tester, database administrator, and so on. The Scrum Development Team is a cross-functional set of such practitioners. It is a myth that the Development Team member must have all of the above skills; it is unrealistic to assume that every Development Team individual can work on every assignment. The Development Team members collectively (i.e., the Development Team) have the skills required to deliver the Product Increment. There are no separate teams like the design team, integration team, testing team, etc. There are no sub-teams in the Development Team.

When forming multiple Scrum teams, the mixture of skills in each team to avoid dependencies on external experts, and the effect of team size on the team's ability to work together should be taken into account.

Only members of the Development Team create the Increment. The Development Team is accountable for the successful delivery of each Sprint Increment.

Development Teams are structured and empowered by the organization to organize and manage their work. The resulting synergy optimizes the Development Team's overall efficiency and effectiveness.

Few points to remember:

- The Development Team members can be changed as needed. If they are changed, then productivity will be reduced for the short-term. Development team members should not be changed, added or removed when the Sprint is in progress; they should be changed, added or removed in between Sprints if needed.

- Scrum Teams for the same product can be increased or decreased. If it is done, the productivity of the original Scrum team usually decreases for a short-term.

Key Responsibilities

- Development Team performs all the work of requirement understanding, designing, coding, integration, testing, documentation, and so on to turn the Product Backlog Items into the Product Increment.

- The Development Team is responsible for conducting Daily Scrum.

- The Development Team is responsible for tracking the progress of the work remaining in the Sprint to achieve the Sprint Goal.

- Development Team is responsible for the Product Backlog Items estimation. Others may try to influence, but the Development Team is the only ultimately responsible for estimation.

- The Development Team resolves the Development Team's impediments and internal conflicts on its own. If no solution is found, reach Scrum Master.

- Development Team creates the Definition of Done (DoD). Development Team can consult the Product Owner for creating the DoD. The Product Owner may influence the creation of DoD, but the Development Team is ultimately accountable.

Development Team Size

The recommended development Team size should be 3 to 9 (excluding the Product Owner and Scrum Master).

Optimal Development Team size is small enough to remain nimble and large enough to complete significant work within a Sprint.

Fewer than three Development Team members decrease interaction and result in smaller productivity gains. Smaller Development Teams may encounter skill constraints during the Sprint, causing the Development Team to be unable to deliver a potentially releasable Increment. Having more than nine members requires too much coordination. Large Development Teams generate too much complexity for an empirical process to be useful.

The Product Owner and Scrum Master roles are not included in this count unless they are also executing the work of the Sprint Backlog.

If team size is less than 3 or higher than 9, does the team do Scrum. Based on thorough research and studies, a range of 3–9 is reached. Teams should be small enough to complete the work (should not have skill constraints or result in lower productivity gains) and large enough to use the empirical process (should not be too complicated to coordinate). Can you say that a team does not do Scrum because they have 10 Developers? If there would be no lower productivity gains in a specific instance by breaking the limit or no complexity for an empirical process to be useful, then different range may hold. The result may be suboptimal.

Characteristics

Development Team have the following characteristics:

- They are self-organizing. No one (not even the Scrum Master) tells the Development Team how to turn Product Backlog into Increments of potentially releasable functionality.

- Development Teams are cross-functional, with all the skills (collectively as a team) to create a product Increment.

- Scrum recognizes no titles for Development Team members, regardless of the work being performed by the person.

- Scrum recognizes no sub-teams in the Development Team, regardless of domains that need to be addressed like testing, architecture, operations, or business analysis.

- Individual Development Team members may have specialized skills and area of focus where Development Team member prefers to work. However, they also works outside of their core specialty area as needed. This is called T-shaped skills – strong specialized skills in the primary area (specialty) and broad skills to work outside of the primary area. The letter "T" is used to describe the expertise of such individuals, with a vertical (trunk) line of the letter, representing the depth of primary skill and horizontal line of the letter, representing the breadth of secondary skills. In contrast, "I-shaped" individuals have only primary skills but no secondary skillset.

- Development Team members collectively own the responsibility of getting the job done. All are responsible as one team for the success and failure of the result. Accountability belongs to the entire Development Team.

- Sprint Backlog belongs to the Development Team. The ownership of the Sprint Backlog Item lies with the entire Development Team and not a particular individual. Only Development Team can update the Sprint Backlog. The Development team informs the Product Owner to work with anyone who requests Development Team to add new PBI to a Sprint that is currently ongoing.

- The Development Team pulls the work from the Product Backlog, and no one should push Product Backlog Items from the Product Backlog to the Development Team.

- Development team members must work at a pace that can be sustained within regular working hours. They focus on delivering valuable working software at a sustainable pace. They deliver value at frequent, regular intervals without working overtime.

- Development team members should be kept together as long as it is f sensible to do so. Long established teams are more productive than the newly formed ones.

Multiple Development Teams

- When forming the new Development Teams, Scrum Master should bring all developers together and let them self-organize into Development Teams. If the existing Development Team needs to organize into the new structure, they propose how they would like to form it.

- Multiple Development Teams when they are working for the same product should minimize the dependencies between the teams. The Development Team member working on multiple Scrum teams at the same time is usually less productive than working on a single Scrum team.

- A scaled Scrum has more than one Scrum Team working from the same Product Backlog. A well-structured Product Backlog minimizes and sometimes eliminate the need of Development Team members working on multiple Scrum teams during a Sprint.

- When multiple Scrum teams are working on the same product, the Development Teams pull the work from a shared Product Backlog in agreement with the Product Owner and the other teams. One Product Backlog helps in synchronizing all the teams working on the same product.

- Development teams are usually formed as feature teams or component teams.

- A feature team has all the skills to complete the Product Backlog Items. A feature team works on multiple application layers (for example, front end, business layer or back end) throughout a Sprint and deliver working software every Sprint.

- A component team address one single layer only. The component team is usually made up of people with similar specialty skills.

- In Scrum, feature teams are preferred. It is a myth that Scrum should not be adopted until teams are moved from component-based to feature teams.

- When moving away from component teams toward feature teams, feature teams require time to become productive as people from the different layers and components get to working and delivering unified functionality together. Productivity may suffer during the transition; however, the delivery of business value would increase.

- Feature teams are favorable as they have less communication overhead.

The Scrum Master

Overview

Scrum Master helps everyone understand the spirit of Scrum. The Scrum Master is accountable for the way Scrum is understood and enacted.

Scrum Master has reasonable technical and domain knowledge. Scrum Master acts as a collaboration conductor to work with the Product Owner, Development Team, and outsiders to the Scrum Team. The Scrum Master is transparent in all forms of communication, and there are no hidden agendas.

The Scrum Master is responsible for ensuring an effective Daily Scrum happens every day and is time-boxed to 15 minutes even though he or she is an optional attendee in the Daily Scrum. Scrum Master ensures that the Development Team has the Daily Scrum and makes sure that the Development Team members participate in it and keep the Daily Scrum within the time-box.

The Scrum Master helps those outside the Scrum Team understand which of their interactions with the Scrum Team are helpful and which are not. The Scrum Master helps everyone change these interactions to maximize the value created by the Scrum Team. The Scrum Master protects the team from people (outsiders to the Scrum Team) with different agendas.

It is a myth that Scrum Master is responsible for hiring and firing of Development team members, or is an administrator who is responsible for providing the required software, or is responsible for writing the notes during Scrum events.

A Scrum Master knows the different phases a Development Team goes through when working as a team - forming, storming, norming, performing, and adjourning.

A Great Scrum Master:

- Takes the problem to the team, instead of solving on behalf of team.

- Remain detached from outcomes in any condition.

- Get comfortable with an uncomfortable silence, wait patiently and let someone else on the team have room to speak.

- Should use her powerful observations and powerful questions during the conversation.

- Knows constructive disagreement should not be avoided, and it can be used to build strong teams. Helps the team move through conflict and live with it if it is unsolvable.

- Should support the Development Team in such a manner that the Development Team does not need Scrum Master anymore daily.

- Shares lessons learned and experiences with others.

- Sets the examples for teams. Team learn how to use Agile well through Scrum Master's example.

Service to the Product Owner

The Scrum Master serves the Product Owner in several ways, including:

- Ensuring that goals, scope, and product domain are understood by everyone on the Scrum Team as well as possible

- Finding techniques for effective Product Backlog management

- Helping the Scrum Team understand the need for clear and concise Product Backlog Items

- Understanding product planning in an empirical environment

- Ensuring the Product Owner knows how to arrange the Product Backlog to maximize value

- Understanding and practicing agility

- Facilitating Scrum events as requested or needed

Service to the Development Team

The Scrum Master serves the Development Team in several ways, including:

- Coaching the Development Team in self-organization and cross-functionality

- Helping the Development Team to create high-value products

- Removing impediments to the Development Team's progress

- Facilitating Scrum events as requested or needed

- Coaching the Development Team in organizational environments in which Scrum is not yet fully adopted and understood

Service to the Organization

The Scrum Master serves the organization in several ways, including:

- Leading and coaching the organization in its Scrum adoption

- Planning Scrum implementations within the organization

- Helping employees and stakeholders understand and enact Scrum and empirical product development

- Causing change that increases the productivity of the Scrum Team

- Working with other Scrum Masters to increase the effectiveness of the application of Scrum in the organization

Key Responsibilities

- Scrum Master teaches Scrum framework (any part of the framework – roles, artifacts, events, etc.) whenever the team goes out of track. Scrum Master teaches enough to convey the lesson without impacting the teams' momentum.

- Scrum Master recognizes how the Scrum Team uses Scrum and makes every effort to help it reach the next level. Scrum Master is a mentor-coach, teacher, facilitator, and much more.

- Scrum Master helps the Scrum team to define and adhere to its own process for making sure the work is done. A great Scrum Master ensures the entire team supports the chosen Scrum process and understands the value of every event. For example, the Daily Scrum is planned at a time that suits all team members.

- Scrum Master is a servant to the Scrum Team whose focus is on the needs of the Scrum Team to achieve the business results.

- Scrum Master, as a mentor, provides guidance and possibly some direction to the Scrum Team as needed.

- The Scrum Master protects the Development Team from outside intrusion so that Development Team can focus on delivering value. For example, if a manager starts participating in Daily Scrum, then Scrum Master protects the Development Team by telling the manager that she can attend the meeting, but she should not participate.

- Scrum Master prefers not to give out the answers. If Development Team members are not able to solve the problem themselves, the Scrum Master's help (do not solve it herself) them to solve their own problems. Scrum Master uses the coaching skills to ask thoughtful, deep, and probing questions (a kind of enquiry) to help the Development Team to find out the answer to their questions (or the problems).

- The Scrum Master takes ownership of resolving the problems if the problem is an impediment that inhibits the Development Team's productivity and Development Team members themselves cannot remove it. The Scrum Master solves blocking issues to the Development Team's progress, taking into account the self-organizing capabilities of the Development Team.

- Scrum Master is a conflict navigator. Scrum Master gives time to the Development Team to resolve his or her own conflicts.

- Scrum Master ensures that effective change is occurring at all levels of the organization. Scrum Master enables a culture in which Scrum Teams can flourish.

Is There a Place for "Managers"?

Managers play an important role, although Scrum does not purposefully have them within a minimal structure.

- Scrum is entirely dependent on the organization's management to build a supportive workplace for Scrum teams.

- The manager handles the operational and logistical requirements of teams.

- In an Agile organization, the manager is still responsible for Scrum team members' personal development. People development is the responsibility of everyone in the organization.

- Scrum Masters facilitate team members to grow while the manager usually facilitates the personal growth of entire teams.

- Managers remove business-related impediments that prevent the optimal functioning of Scrum teams.

How Testing is Different in Scrum Project?

Testing used to be a phase in the traditional way of working, which means testing could not be done before the development phase is finished. In Scrum projects, testing is not a phase. Testing is more of an activity that can be done all the time throughout the Sprint. Even testing can start from beginning if you are following the test-first approach like Test-Driven Development.

In traditional way of working, there is a mindset that tester has to find and log as many numbers of bugs as possible to prove that he or she has achieved targets of finding bugs. Instead, now everyone needs to adapt to prevent the bugs approach.

Job of checking the specification is fulfilled or not should be given to the machines. Hence, automation testing is preferred nowadays. In order to adopt shorter iteration Sprints, automation testing should be considered to reduce the testing time.

Testing should be considered as a mindset to find new ideas, to find different use cases, and to find any hidden assumptions. Earlier approach of breaking the system should be shifted to the approach of helping to build the best system. Hence, team collaboration is essential.

Old thinking of only tester is responsible for quality should be changed. In the traditional way of working, we used to say earlier that developers cannot be trusted for quality. Everyone should adopt the direction that the whole team takes responsibility for quality.

Sample Questions

Q: In a MNC organization, a Scrum project started with two weeks Sprint and 7 developers. Four month are completed, team is enjoying their work and successfully delivering the Product Increment. In the middle of the 9th Sprint, Sales Department Head (who is one of the board member) requested Development Team to work on a task that is important and needed for the organization. The Development team referred him to the Product Owner Carlos. Scrum Master Meisa was observing all what was happening. What do you think Meisa should have done?

1. Team did the right thing, Meisa should do nothing
2. As Scrum recommends, Scrum Master can also be part of Development Team. Hence, Meisa should work on such task which is important to organization
3. Mentor Development Team to support top senior management's need as Scrum Team will exist if organization exist
4. Should ask senior management to increase the salary of Developers so that developers will be motivated and can take additional work
5. Both 2 & 3

Q: Development Team decide on how to accomplish their work, and do not depend on others outside the team. Do you agree? Yes or No

Q: Can you help yourself in identifying one important feature of a Development Team?

1. Team should have all the skills necessary to carry out the work without depending on others that are not part of the team
2. Team should be flexible to work overtime and sometime on weekends as working shippable Product Increment should be delivered every Sprint
3. All developers must work from the same location

4. All of the above

5. None of the above

Q: Architecture is an ongoing and continuing activity. Scrum suggests it is not required to develop architecture completely in the first Sprint. Let me know your thoughts. Agree or Disagree

Q: Development Team was discussing on how to manage time spent on impediments while working on the Sprint. One developer Salman suggested creating sub-teams that way they can maintain high utilization of resources and remain productive when impediments occur. Do you agree? True or False

Q: The Scrum Master has no authority on the developers and their aspirations. True or False

Q: Product Owner can be a single person or a small committee of people. True or False

Q: Who is responsible for maximizing the value of the product?

1. Scrum Master

2. Development Team

3. Scrum Team

4. Scrum Master and Key Stakeholders

5. Product Owner

6. Product Value Maximizer

Q: Sometime Scrum Master can change the effort estimate done by Development Team if it benefits to project. True or False

Q: Select the responsibilities of the Product Owner from following. Select all applicable

1. Maximize the value of the product

2. Causing change that increases the productivity of the Scrum Team

3. Maximize the value of the work done by the Development Team
4. Change effort estimate done by Development Team, only if Scrum Master asks for so
5. Successful delivery of each Sprint Increment

Q: An Agile Coach Haruka in one Scrum session said Scrum Master can be considered as a management position as the Scrum Master is accountable for following management activities. Can you select all applicable?

1. For managing the delivery plan
2. For managing the utilization of the developers
3. For managing the Scrum process
4. For managing the Product Owner

Q: As per Scrum, one Scrum Master can manage at most one Scrum Team at a time. True or False

Q: The Product Owner is responsible for the product, hence, the Product Owner regulates which developer is needed in which Development Team based on their skills & experience so that they can generate more value. True or False

Q: Scrum Master is a conflict resolver; hence, Scrum Master shifts developers from one team to other as needed. True or False

Q: Development Teams are created by providing developers boundaries to organize themselves as Development Team. True or False

Q: Scrum is flexible; in some cases, based on the complexity of the project, it allows Development Teams to have different roles like UI designers, Testers, Database Designer, etc. True or False

Q: The best size for a Development Team is six people. True or False

Q: Who facilitates Scrum events?

1. Development Team

2. Product Owner

3. Scrum Master

4. Anyone whose bandwidth is available

5. Event facilitator team at organization level

Q: Who track the total work remaining at least in the Daily Scrum?

1. Scrum Master

2. Product Owner

3. Development Team

4. All of the above

5. Tracking is Waterfall approach; no one does tracking in Scrum.

Q: Couple of years ago, Mary had worked as a senior developer in one of the software development project in the organization. Now she is the Product Owner for a Scrum project. She is attending the Daily Scrum to track each developer's daily work. She started asking status to each developer; developers were not sure what to do in that situation and hence started providing the progress report to Mary. What should Scrum Master Jimmy do?

1. Scrum is the solution to complex problems. Do nothing

2. Scrum Master is a higher role than the Product Owner. Hence, Jimmy asks Development Team to start reporting to him instead of Mary.

3. Like an Agile Coach, coach the whole Scrum Team on purpose of Scrum events and let the team find their way

4. Jimmy should talk to Mary and enquire what makes her interesting attend the Daily Scrum and ask her to stop attending Daily Scrum.

Q: Whom does Scrum Master serve? Select all applicable

1. Product Owner

2. Organization

3. Stakeholders

4. Development Team

Q: Product Owner Alex is maximizing the value of the product. She chooses and manages the Product Backlog with her understanding. She does not take into account stakeholder's desires. Do you think Alex is doing right thing? True or False

Q: Scrum Master does not have direct control over the team's work. True or False

Q: Scrum Master does not have direct control over the team's work, but is still responsible for its results. True or False

Q: Product Owner always works with senior developers to order Product Backlog Items as they have good technical knowledge and one more benefit is other developers can focus and utilize their time for the product development. True or False

Q: During Sprint, the Product Owner should interact with the Development Team to enhance the value of the work performed by development. How does a Scrum Master understand about this interaction? Select all applicable

1. Scrum Master observes Sprint Review meeting and will see if the Product Owner is satisfied with presentation of the team and value of Increment

2. Scrum Master asks Development Team to send weekly report to monitor this interaction

3. Development Team is self-organized. Scrum Master should not do anything

4. Scrum Master observes Sprint Planning meeting and will see if the Product Owner is sharing required information to the Development Team

Q: If the Scrum Master is part of the Development Team, then the maximum number of allowed members in the Development Team is 10. True or False

Q: Scrum Master is viewed as a management position since Scrum Master is accountable for eliminating organizational obstacles that restrict the advancement of the team. True or False

Q: In one Scrum project of 7 developers, some have deep specialized skills in programming, and few have testing skills and few in UI designing. Development Team has T-shaped skills. User documentation is part of their definition of Done. However, the Development Team does not have technical writers. Organization also do not have anyone to make available for Development Team. The HR team has started the process of hiring technical writers. Which of the following statements is true.

1. Development Team should ask Scrum Master to do the documentation until organization provides them the technical writers.

2. Scrum suggests working software over documentation. Keep user documentation on low priority than developing software entirely. If Developers get the time after developing software, they can contribute to documentation as a self-organization team.

3. Definition of Done is a checklist of the types of work that the Development is expected to complete before it can declare Product Increment to be potentially shippable. Hence, Development is responsible for writing user documentation, and they will write it.

4. Inform management that it is management's responsibility to provide technical writers to the Development Team. Development Team is not responsible if they cannot provide technical writers on time to the Development Team.

Q: If the Product Owner is part of the Development Team, then the maximum number of allowed members in the Development Team is 10. True or False

Q: A new Scrum Master Carmelita with 6 months of work experience has just joined the organization. A senior Scrum Master Frank was discussing in general with Carmelita in a common platform that a Scrum Master is accountable for the way Scrum is understood and enacted. Frank suggested few points to Carmelita, can you identify what would be those from the following list? Select all applicable

1. Scrum Master should blame Product Owner if teams are not understanding the Scrum.
2. A Scrum Master should take one on one coaching sessions as necessary to address any issues found.
3. A Scrum Master should plan the trainings for team.
4. Scrum Master should blame the organization teams are not understanding the Scrum.
5. Scrum Master is not accountable for the way Scrum is understood and enacted.

Q: Scrum framework ensures that adding more developers to a Scrum project equally increases the value delivered. True or False

Q: In a MNC, a new Scrum Team is formed with 8 developers. 10 Sprints are completed successfully. Suddenly, few developers started coming late to Daily Scrum by a couple of minutes (approximately 3 to 4 minutes). As everyone knows, if corrective actions are not taken on time, slowly it becomes practice. Same thing happened in this team. Because of this, developers are not able to complete Daily Scrum in 15 minutes. They approached their Scrum Master Catherine for her advice. What do you think Catherine should do? Select all applicable.

1. The manager is responsible for the personal development of the members of a Development Team. Catherine should ask the Development Team to improve else, she should inform their managers.

2. Catherine should start a penalty system. The developer will have to pay a $1 if he or she comes late. The collected amount will be used to buy the treat for the Scrum Team.

3. Be an Agile Coach; ask the question to the Development Team that what they think should be done to ensure their Daily Scrum is effective.

4. Catherine should advise Development Team to try something new and move the Daily Scrum to a time that suits the Development team.

5. All of the above.

Q: In a startup organization Fortaleza SoftTech, a Development Team of 6 developers were working on a Scrum Project from last 6 months. On one day, the intense argument between the two developers Jermaine and Ranbir was observed by Scrum Master Serena. They were each other insulting. They were discussing on the tasks that were not accomplished. Few developers were supporting Jermaine's view and few others Ranbir's view. It was a very uncomfortable situation for everyone. Serena should remove them from the team, with the help of their managers and HR team. True or False

Q: Five Scrum Teams are working on the one product. What do you think about the selection of Product Backlog Items?

1. All Scrum Masters from each team meets and decides the order in which their teams should select the PBIs.

2. The Product Owner provides Product Backlog to each Scrum team.

3. Each Development team takes an equal number of PBIs.

4. Each Development Team pull the PBIs in agreement with the Product Owner and the other teams.

Q: Management of PentaZone Corp has assigned Misty as the Scrum Master of three new Scrum teams to build one product. Select all applicable.

1. Scrum does not recommend anything, PentaZone may decide on how much Product Owners and Product Backlogs are needed.
2. There should be separate Product Owner for each Scrum Team. Three Product Owners are needed.
3. There should be separate Product Backlog for each Scrum Team
4. This product has one Product Backlog.
5. There should be only one Product Owner.

Q: Can you select one major issue of various Development Teams when they work from the same Product Backlog?

1. Interpersonal issues of the developers from the multiple Development Teams
2. Minimizing dependencies between Development Teams
3. Minimizing dependencies between Product Owners
4. Make sure that every team has enough work for each developer

Q: Scrum Master Allyson has asked 70 developers to form multiple Scrum Teams. Can you suggest what factors should be considered when developers are forming into multiple Scrum teams? Select all applicable

1. The combination of senior or junior developers on each Development Team
2. Equal distribution of Scrum Masters in each Development Team
3. The combination of skills in each Development Team to avoid dependencies on outside members
4. Equal distribution of testers in each Development Team

Q: In DietAlmera Corp, Development Teams are organized to address a single layer. One team for UI layer, other for business layer, and another for database layer. Agile coach Rebecca and teams were discussing to move away from layered (component) teams to feature teams. Select all applicable

1. Productivity may suffer from this type of change for some duration
2. Feature teams will always have more velocity than component team
3. Feature teams have fewer overhead communication
4. Features teams are more self-organized than layered teams

Q: A new developer Ranveer asked, who ensures that the Development Team knows the Product Backlog Items to the required level?

1. Scrum Master
2. Product Owner
3. Key Stakeholders
4. Agile Coach

Q: The Scrum Team consists of. Select all applicable

1. Product Owner
2. Key Stakeholders
3. Development Team Member
4. Testing Team Member
5. Scrum Master

Q: A new developer Masaki wanted to know who should be responsible for monitoring the remaining project work towards the project goal? Can you help him to find out the answer? Select all applicable

1. Scrum Master
2. Product Owner
3. Developer's Supervisor
4. Development Team

Q: Three Development Teams working on the same product must have same Scrum Master. True or False

Q: Product Owner Sota was thinking if it is mandatory for him to attend Sprint Retrospective. Do you think it is mandatory? Yes or No

Q: Developers are self-organized and should work on their own, and do not require a manager to handle the Sprint activities for them. True or False

Q: The Development Team is collectively accountable for delivering the Product Increment; however, it is the responsibility of the senior members of the team to ensure its success.

Q: A junior developer who is recently joined a Scrum Team asks one question that who should ensure that the Product Backlog is visible and clear to all. What would be your answer?

1. Scrum Master
2. Product Owner
3. Development Team
4. Product Backlog Master

Q: A Senior Manager Dave asked one question on Scrum in their board meeting. Is it true that if Scrum is implemented properly, managers are no longer required? What do you think? Yes or No

Q: A new IT Manager who is new to Scrum wants to understand who chooses if the Development Team has enough skills to generate shippable Product Increment.

1. Scrum Master
2. Product Owner
3. Scrum Lead
4. Development Team
5. Human Resources Team

Q: Could the Product Owner and the Scrum Master be a part of the Development Team? Yes or No

Q: Can you select the correct statement about a Product Owner?

1. Product Owner is similar to a project lead
2. Focus on the delivery and not the quality, as quality can be improved in subsequent builds
3. Typically get business value delivered early and frequently
4. Should have experience as a developer in the past

Q: Scrum has a role called Project Manager whose responsibility is on-boarding and off-boarding the developers as per project need. True or False

Q: The Scrum Master mainly focus on the Scrum Team and generally not concerned with those outside the Scrum Team. True or False

Q: Product Owner can add or remove Product Backlog Item from the Product Backlog and can change their priority at any moment, as Scrum is about responding quickly to change .True or False

Q: How does the Scrum Master help the Product Owner? Select all applicable

1. Understanding product planning in an empirical environment
2. Facilitating Scrum events as requested or needed
3. Finding techniques for effective Product Backlog management
4. Scrum Master is not supposed to help anyone

Q: Bretagne InfoTech has won a project and going to kick start the project in one month. They have 11 associates, some are developers and some are testers. Apart from these associates, they have Jackie as a Scrum Master and Ajay as the Product Owner. How will Jackie distribute associates between Development Teams?

1. Two teams of 6 and 5 people. The associates decides this option after a short meeting
2. Three Development Teams of 4, 4 and 3 people. All Development Team are cross-functional

3. One team of developers and other team of testers

4. Both 1 & 2

Q: Who determines whether the Development Team has been assigned enough work in a Sprint?

1. The Development Team

2. The Product Owner

3. The Product Owner and the Scrum Master

4. The Scrum Master

Q: Can you select one primary responsibility of the Scrum Master?

1. Approve the estimation done by developers

2. Remove any obstacles encountered by the Development Team during their work

3. Work with the Product Owner to develop the Product Backlog

4. Supervisor of the Development Team

Q: A Scrum project with 2 weeks Sprint has completed 9 Sprints. In the mid of the 10th Sprint, a Development Team determines that it will not be able to finish the selected Product Backlog Items. Who should all be present to review and adjust the Sprint work selected?

1. Scrum Master & Product Owner

2. The Product Owner and the Development Team.

3. The Product Owner and all stakeholders.

4. The Development Team.

Q: A Scrum Team of 5 developers, one Scrum Master Mithali and one Product Owner Aaryan are defining the Product Backlog Items. Mithali notices that the Development Team is not using the User Story format to write the PBIs. What do you suggest Mithali should do?

1. Ask Development Team for not complying with the user stories format.

2. Mithali should allow the Development Team to decide the format of Product Backlog Items.
3. Add one technical writer in Development Team for writing user stories.
4. Mithali should inform to Product Owner that Development is not following the user story format.

Q: The Manager is still responsible for the personal development of Scrum team members in an Agile organization. True or False

Q: Scrum Master ensures that the Development Team has the Daily Scrum meeting. True or False

Q: What does the Scrum Master do about the Daily Scrum?

1. Is responsible for conducting the Daily Scrum
2. Teaches the Development Team to keep the Daily Scrum within the 20-minute time-box
3. If others are present at the Daily Scrum, make sure that they do not interfere with the meeting
4. All of the above

Q: Scrum Master serve the organization by working with other Scrum Masters to strengthen the efficiency of Scrum's implementation in the organization. True or False

Q: Scrum Master serve the organization by working with other Product Owners (for different products) to strengthen the efficiency of Scrum's implementation in the organization. True or False

Q: How does the Scrum Master serve the organization? Select all applicable

1. Planning implementation of the Scrum within the organization
2. Coaching the organization in its Scrum adoption
3. By taking additional part time role to remove impediments at organization level
4. All of the above

Q: Maintaining the Product Backlog is not a Product Owner's responsibility. True or False

Q: Which of the following is not a Product Owner responsibility? Select all applicable

1. Giving the inputs to the Development Team to select a set of Product Backlog Items
2. Assigning tasks to team members
3. Prioritizing the Product Backlog
4. On-boarding developers as per project need

Q: Scrum Master is responsible for setting priorities together with Product Owner for Product Backlog Items. True or False

Q: Which of the following is Scrum Master's responsibility? Select all applicable

1. Prevention of changing team priorities by senior management
2. Ensuring that effective change is occurring at all levels of the organization
3. Helping the Development Team to create high-value products
4. Coaching the organization in its Scrum adoption

Q: If all teams follows the same release schedule, it will ensures the frequent delivery of value to the customer. True or False

Q: A new Scrum Master Lorna joined the organization for one Scrum project. Lorna wanted to know if she should be present daily at the Daily Scrum. Can you tell me the main reason for the Lorna to attend the Daily Scrum?

1. Lorna can ensure that each member of the Development Team answers the three questions.
2. Lorna does not have to attend Daily Scrum; she only has to ensure that the Development Team has a Daily Scrum.

3. Lorna can jot down the action items identified in the Daily Scrum.

4. Lorna can ask Product Owner in Daily Scrum if there are any open issues without waiting any longer.

Q: A Senior developer Anderson said Managers make good Scrum Masters because they already have experience of organizing and running the teams. Do you agree with Anderson? Yes or No

Q: What does Product Backlog management include?

1. Optimizing the value of the work the Development Team performs

2. Ensuring that the Product Backlog is visible, transparent, and clear to all, and shows what the Scrum Team will work on next

3. Ordering the items in the Product Backlog to best achieve goals and missions

4. All of the above

Q: A senior developer Anthony said, Managers make good Product Owners as they already have experience that requires decision making and directing the teams. What is your opinion? True or False

Q: Product Owners are specialists in their domain and create a powerful connection with stakeholders over a period of time. Hence, changing the Product Owners across the Scrum teams frequently is regarded as effective. Do you agree? Yes or No.

Q: An organization CologneCorp has won a complex project (received purchase order for 1 year i.e. budget is available for 1 year) and need to kick start it. Multiple Scrum Teams will be needed to execute this project. Which of the following statements is true.

1. Scrum is easy to understand, challenging to master and is not for a complex project.

2. Initially, start with one or two teams of best developers, add more teams later.

3. All teams should be added upfront so that all developers will be on the same page.

4. Start with 1 team and after 10th month add four teams.

Q: Scrum project with 5 developers, one Scrum Master Victoria, one Product Owner Prabhas is running successfully from last two months. However, in one Sprint, stakeholders noted during the Sprint Review that progress in product development is not very obviously noticeable and appears to lack transparency. Can you help yourself to answer who is responsible for this situation?

1. Chief Stakeholder

2. Prabhas

3. Development Team

4. Victoria

Q: Can you tell me what is enough to start the first Sprint?

1. Developers, UI designers, one tester should be available from the start. Remaining testers can be added before completing development phase.

2. A first Sprint requires no more than a Product Owner, a Development Team, and enough ideas to complete a full Sprint.

3. A finalized Product Backlog so that all requirements are clear upfront

4. Architecture should be finalized

5. None of the above

Q: Product Owner Siddhesh should consult with main stakeholders when considering the value of a Product. True or False

Q: In a newly formed Scrum team, a developer Yudai asked is Scrum Master a "Management" position. True or False

Q: Product Owners can delegate some of their work to others. Can you select some of the following items which Product Owner might delegate. Select all applicable

1. Ordering PB
2. Writing user stories
3. Attending Sprint Review meetings
4. None of the above

Q: Product Owner always looks to maximize the value of the product. Product Owner focus on following things to ensure his product delivers the value. Select all applicable

1. Closely monitoring the team during testing phase
2. Stakeholder Participation
3. Product Marketplace
4. Product Release Decisions
5. Closely monitoring the team during entire Sprint

Q: Who can decide if the Product Increment should be released or not?

1. Release Team
2. Product Owner
3. Scrum Master
4. Development Team
5. Product Sponsor and Board of Management

Q: Product Owner can delegate the writing of all of the Product Backlog Items to the Development Team. True or False

Q: What are the responsibilities of a self-organizing Development Team? Select all applicable.

1. Update the daily progress to stakeholders
2. Increase in velocity
3. Reorder the Product Backlog.

4. All of the above

5. None of the above

Q: The Product Owner must write all Product Backlog Items before starting the first Sprint? True or False

Q: One of the department of organization started adopting Agile, department head should protect their Scrum teams from uncertainty formed by other departments whose associates do not know Scrum yet and not started adopting Agile. True or False

Q: Product Owner Saina was telling her colleagues about her job duties as a Product Owner. She told them that she has to focus on some of the following things. Select all applicable

1. Writing Product Backlog Items

2. Publishing Product Increment release status with all stakeholders

3. Participating in the Daily Scrum meetings

4. Development may need her for requirement clarification, hence, being with the Development Team all the time

Q: Agile is recently adopted in RabatCorp. In one of the training session, IT manager asked how long Development Teams should be kept together in Scrum. Other member in the session replied, members of the Development Team should be maintained together as long as it is financially sustainable to do so. Long-lasting Development Teams are more efficient than new teams. Do you also agree with this? True or False

Q: How does Scrum Master ensure effective communication between the Development Team and the Product Owner?

1. By tracking communications between the Development Team and the Product Owner and facilitate direct collaboration

2. By observing interaction between Development Team and Product Owner in Daily Scrum meetings

3. As the Development Team is self-organizing, Scrum Master should not to do anything

4. All of the above

Q: In a small organization, a Scrum team of 8 members is working on a product from last 1 year. Two more Scrum teams are added for developing that product, what will be the instant impact on the productivity of the Scrum Team of 8 members?

1. Productivity would probably remain same

2. Productivity would probably increase

3. Productivity would probably decrease

4. Productivity would probably start increasing as complexity of product decreases

Q: A new developer Rodrigo once asked to the Development Team what belongs solely to us out of the following. Select all applicable.

1. The Sprint Backlog

2. Definition of Done

3. User Stories

4. All of the above

Q: Do you think the Product Owner has the authority to replace an item in the Sprint Backlog. True or false?

Q: The Project Manager Vijay requested Scrum Master Kanchan to provide status report about the progress. What should she do?

1. Kanchan prepares the status report herself and shares with Vijay

2. Kanchan asks Development Team to send report to Vijay and every developer should get a change on rotation basis to send the report to the Manager

3. Kanchan asks senior developer to send the report to Vijay

4. Kanchan says Vijay that status will be visible during the Sprint Review
5. None of the above

Q: All Scrum teams must have a Product Owner and Scrum Master.

1. False
2. True and productivity and progress depends on their availability
3. Depends on an organization
4. True and they should be available 100% dedicated to the Scrum Team

Q: In a Pune based organization; a new Scrum team of 8 members is formed for developing a new product. The Development Team was not clear on how to plan the task for the Product Backlog Items chosen for the Sprint. Development Team contacted Scrum Master Danica for her advice. What should Danica do?

1. Danica should ask the Development Team to figure out themselves
2. She should take one session on Scrum for the Development Team
3. She should take help from other Scrum Team in the organization
4. She should inform Project Manager about inabilities of the Development Team so that Project Manager can give feedback to the developers during appraisal discussion

Q: Product Owner Brigitte is working with ItsukushimaCorp from last 10 years. She was working on one new product as a Product Owner from last one year. 7 developers were working and Sprint duration was two weeks. In one particular Sprint after one week, Brigitte comes to Scrum Master Ronaldo and tells that she feels like the Development Team will not be able to finish all selected Product Backlog Items. Hence, Ronaldo added more developers to the Development Team so that the Development Team can complete all PBIs on time. Do you agree with Ronaldo? Yes or No

Q: During the refinement meeting Development Team discussed on one of the top Product Backlog Item that has dependency on a part developed by another Development Team which is under development. Development Team has taken that PBI into the next Sprint. Do you think what Development Team did is correct? Yes or No

Q: In a startup organization Vaikuntha SoftTech, 9 members Scrum team started working on a Product. Six Sprints were completed successfully. Development Team has a combination of junior and senior developers. Developer Hilary loves to talk on project design all the time and she always discuss on the task implemented by other developers and then design followed for that task implementation. She was spending several hours in such discussions. Some of the developers got frustrated. After three more Sprints, few developers complained Scrum Master Ronaldo about Hilary. What should Ronaldo do?

1. Ronaldo should replace Hilary with some other developer.
2. Ronaldo should discuss with Hilary and ask her to act as a team player.
3. Inform Hilary's Manager to provide this feedback to Hilary in the appraisal discussion.
4. Ask Development Team to discuss with Product Owner about Hilary and figure it out solution to this problem.

Q: Product Owner Lisa is working with Aundha InfoTech. Organization has asked Lisa to work on a new product with multiple Development Teams. Lisa is aware of the fact that when multiple teams are involved dependencies between teams must be minimized. How will Lisa achieve it?

1. Lisa asks Project Manager to coach Development Team to identify dependencies between PBIs
2. Lisa asks Scrum Master to work with Development Team to minimize the PBI dependencies
3. As Lisa is aware that dependencies will always exist between multiple teams, she will reorder the PBIs and move on.

4. Lisa works with the Development Teams to form a Product Backlog to minimize dependencies between Scrum Teams.

Q: Scrum recognizes no sub-teams in the Development Team. True or False

Q: There was one Scrum Team working on a product. A new Scrum team was added to work on the same product. Which of the following statements are true about the first team?

1. Productivity would probably remain same
2. Productivity would probably increase
3. Productivity would probably decrease
4. None of the above

Q: During the Sprint, the Scrum Master's role is to help the Development Team to create high-value products. True or False

Q: During a Sprint Retrospective, for what is the Scrum Master responsible?

1. To facilitate and participate as a senior team member.
2. Scrum Master does not participate in Sprint Retrospective
3. To facilitate and participate as a Scrum team member.
4. Scrum is not responsible for anything in Sprint Retrospective

Q: In a Development Team of 9 members, a new Developer Lebron joins the team. What should Scrum Master Brian do?

1. Brian should inform Product Owner about the increased team count
2. Brian instructs the Development Team to form two teams, and allow them to decide the appropriate team size
3. Brian should not do anything. The Development Team must fix its own issues
4. Brian raises the increased team size as a probable impediment and help the Development Team decide what to do about it

Q: Choose two responsibilities of a self-organizing Development Team.

1. Do the work planned in the Sprint Backlog
2. Increase in velocity
3. Pull Product Backlog Items for the Sprint
4. Reorder the Product Backlog

Q: What are the primary characteristics of the Scrum team model? Select all applicable

1. Flexibility
2. Creativity
3. Inspection
4. Productivity
5. Transparency
6. Adaptation

Q: Scrum Master helps the Product Owner by facilitating Scrum events as requested or needed. True or False

Q: Maharathi Pvt Ltd won a new project (value $3 Millions) that needed to be developed in Agile. Scrum was adopted, a Development Team of 7 members, Scrum Master Steve and the Product Owner Stephen started working on the project. Development Team has delivered a shippable product Increment. Stephen gave his go-ahead to deploy the increment on production server. However, when Key Stakeholder Maya started using the product she found that product's performance is slow. She complained to the Stephen. Stephen said to Maya that he will verify and update her soon. When Stephen tested the product, he also found slow performance issue. Stephen talks to Steve about the issue. Steve know the ownership of Definition of Done is with Development Team. What do you think, what should Steve do?

1. Steve asks Stephen to discuss with Development Team so that the Development Team can include more stringent criteria in Definition of Done for achieving higher performance.

2. Steve and Stephen should wait until a Retrospective meeting, as the Development Team will re-consider the Definition of Done in the Retrospective and includes more stringent criteria for higher performance.

3. Do nothing. The Development Team has to decide on acceptable performance criteria.

4. Steve coaches Maya on Scrum processes and ask her to collaborate with Development Team.

Q: Scrum recognizes no titles for Development Team members. True or False

Q: What does Product Backlog management include? Select all applicable

5. Reordering the Product Backlog Items during Daily Scrum

6. Moving Product Backlog Items into the Sprint Backlog

7. Presenting Product Backlog Items to the Key Stakeholders

8. Optimizing the value of the work the Development Team performs

Q: Scrum Master acts as a proxy when the Product Owner is not available to the team. True or False

Q: Who is responsible for promoting and supporting Scrum?

1. The Development Team

2. HR Team

3. Scrum Promoting Team

4. The Scrum Team

Q: How does the Scrum Master serve the Development Team? Select all applicable

1. Removing impediments to the Development Team's progress

2. Adding or removing developers from the Development Team as needed

3. Helping the Development Team to create high-value products
4. Helping Development Team to use tools, processes, and techniques approved by the Organization
5. None of the above

Q: How does the Scrum Master serve the organization? Select all applicable.

1. Adding or removing developers from the Development Team as needed
2. Working with other Scrum Masters in the organization to increase the effectiveness of the application of Scrum in the organization
3. Ensure that the important stakeholders are invited to all Scrum Reviews within the organization
4. None of the above

Q: Who is responsible for tracking the total work remaining in a Sprint?

1. The Product Owner
2. The Scrum Team
3. The Development Team
4. The Scrum Master
5. No one is responsible

Q: Who is responsible for managing the incomplete transparency of artifact?

1. The Product Owner
2. The Scrum Team
3. The Development Team
4. The Scrum Master
5. No one is responsible

Q: The Development Team should be able to explain to the Product Owner and Scrum Master how it intends to work as a self-organizing team to accomplish the Sprint Goal and create the anticipated Increment at the beginning of the Sprint. True or False

Q: Development Team should possess following essential features. Select all applicable

1. Development Team should complete the committed work planned for the Sprint even if some team members are on leaves
2. Development Team should have all competencies needed to accomplish the work without depending on others outside the team
3. Development Team should decide how best to accomplish their work, rather than being directed by others outside the team
4. Development Team should provide weekly update to all stakeholders

Q: Product Owner manages the project and ensures that the work meets the commitments given to the stakeholders. True or False

Q: How can 10 developers be divided into teams? Select all applicable

1. One team of 6 developers and other team of 4 developers. All Developers has discussed and decided this option
2. One team of 6 developers and other team of 4 testers
3. One team of 10 developers. No need to divide.
4. Three teams of 4, 3 and 3 developers.

Q: Scrum Master Facilitate Daily Scrum in a way that ensures each team member has a chance to speak. True or False.

Q: What are the characteristics of a Development Team? Select two

1. All are developers in Development Team
2. Accountability belongs to the Development Team as a whole
3. Inexperienced developers should not be taken in Scrum Development Team as Product Owner monitor the daily progress
4. Scrum Master can perform the role of tester in Development Team

Q: Scrum Master helps the Product Owner by leading and coaching the organization in its Scrum adoption. True or False

Q: How does the Scrum Master helps the Product Owner? Select all applicable

1. Adding or removing developers from the Development Team as needed
2. Understanding product planning in an empirical environment
3. Finding techniques for effective Product Backlog management
4. Scrum Master also perform the role of backup of Product Owner so that when Product Owner is absent Scrum Master can answer the queries of Development Team

Q: Scrum Master should perform following activities about the Daily Scrum. Select all applicable

1. Ensure that all 3 questions have been answered
2. Ensure Product Owner join Daily Scrum on time
3. Teach the Development Team to keep the Daily Scrum within the 15-minute time-box
4. All of the above

Q: Who should understand the most about the progress toward a business goal?

1. The Product Owner
2. The Development Team
3. Business Relationship Manager (BRM)
4. The Scrum Master
5. Scrum Team as a whole

Q: Who is responsible for managing the progress of work during a Sprint?

1. The Development Team
2. Project Manager

3. The Scrum Master
4. The Product Owner
5. All of the above

Q: Which statement best describes a Product Owner's responsibility?

1. Optimizing the value of the work the Development Team does.
2. Managing the Sprint Backlog.
3. Optimizing the value of the work the Scrum Master does.
4. Removing impediments to the Development Team's progress

Q: The CEO of a startup organization Samrajya InfoTech asks the Development Team to add an essential item to a Sprint that is in progress. What do you think the Development Team should do? Select all applicable

1. CEO is giving salary to all employees; hence, his request should be taken on priority. Add the item to the Sprint Backlog and remove some other item from Sprint Backlog.
2. Inform CEO that his request will be taken on priority in next Sprint.
3. Inform the Product Owner so that he can work with the CEO
4. Inform the Scrum Master so that he can work with the CEO
5. Both 1 & 4

Q: What is the recommended size for a Development Team (within the Scrum Team)?

1. As per project complexity
2. 3 to 9
3. 7 plus or minus 2
4. 2 to 10

Q: Magnus a new developer who has just joined the organization has joined one Scrum Team. Magnus understood that Development Tem have all skills collectively. However, he wanted to know why the Development Team should have all the skills needed internally within the team. Help yourself to answer Magnus question. Select all applicable.

1. To turn the Product Backlog Items it selects into an Increment of potentially releasable Product Increment
2. Turn the Sprint Backlog into an Increment of potentially releasable Product Increment
3. Development Team can manage their work even if any developer goes on long vacations for entire Sprint
4. Both 1 and 2

Q: Who should allocate work to the team?

1. Team members should self-select tasks to their priorities and objectives
2. The Scrum Master should allocate tasks to Development Team members
3. The Project Lead should allocate tasks to Development Team members
4. The Product Owner gives clear directives to the team about what they should do and how
5. None of the above

Q: Scrum empowers the team members within appropriate limits. True or False

Q: Self-organizing team encourages an environment of competition and personal advantage. True or False

Q: During the Sprint, the Scrum Master's role is to facilitate inspection and adaptation opportunities as requested or needed. True or False

Q: The Development Team can change its engineering practices whenever they want. True or False

Q: Which of the following statement is true? Select all applicable

1. Scrum Master is a management position. An individual with a powerful knowledge in project leadership and management experience in delivering results is a great fit.
2. Product Owner should perform the role of Scrum Master if budget is the constraints
3. Scrum Master is required only for the half duration of Product development.
4. Scrum Master is the middleman between the Product Owner and the Development Team.

Q: Scrum Master serve Product Owner in following way. Select all applicable

1. By helping the Product Owner to find techniques for managing the Product Backlog
2. By approving the vacations of Product Owner
3. By planning Scrum implementations within the organization
4. None of the above

Q: Who supports the Scrum Master in removing impediments? Select two

1. The Product Owner
2. The senior management
3. Development Team
4. Key Stakeholders

Q: What is the role of Management in Scrum?

1. Monitor the Product Owner's productivity.
2. Monitor the Development Team's productivity.
3. Identify people that are not working beyond office hours.
4. All of the above

Q: Who creates the Sprint Goal?

1. The Development Team
2. The Scrum Master
3. The Scrum Team
4. The Product Owner

Q: The Manager is responsible for the quality of the product in an Agile organization. True or False

Q: The Product Owner is responsible for getting all stakeholders to agree on what provides the most value as Development Team should not spend their time in doing this activity (they should focus on development). True or False

Q: Product Owner should freeze the Product Backlog and should not change it. True or False

Q: The Product Owner should give the Product Backlog to the Development Team and leave the team alone until the intermediate shipment of the Product Increment. True or False

Chapter 7

The Sprint

Overview

In Scrum, work is done in iterations, and these iterations are called Sprints. The goal of each Sprint is to deliver a piece of working software, an Increment of the product, and the Development Team focus on achieving the Sprint Goal.

Sprint is a time-box of one month or less during which potentially shippable product Increment is created. Sprints must be short. A Sprint's duration typically takes one to four weeks, but nothing stops if someone uses Sprint length as one or two days as per the needs. Scrum does not stop you from going with more than one-month Sprint length, but it increases complexity, reduces focus, and delays getting valuable feedback from the stakeholders.

Sprints have consistent durations throughout a development effort. A new Sprint starts immediately after the conclusion of the previous Sprint.

Sprints contain and consist of the Sprint Planning, Daily Scrums, the development work, the Sprint Review, and the Sprint Retrospective. Sprint execution is one of the activities that occur during the Sprint, along with Sprint Planning, Daily Scrum, Sprint Review, and Sprint Retrospective.

During the Sprint:

- No changes are made that would endanger the Sprint Goal.

- Quality goals do not decrease.

- The scope may be clarified and re-negotiated between the Product Owner and Development Team as more is learned.

Each Sprint may be considered a project with no more than a one-month horizon. Like projects, Sprints are used to accomplish something. Each Sprint has a goal of what is to be built, a design and flexible plan that guides building it, the work, and the resultant Product Increment.

Sprints are limited to one calendar month. When a Sprint's horizon is too long, the definition of what is being built may change, complexity may rise, and risk may increase.

Sprints enable predictability by ensuring inspection and adaptation of progress toward a Sprint Goal at least every calendar month. Sprints also limit risk to one calendar month of cost.

- As a rule, no changes should be made which would endanger the Sprint Goal, be it through making changes in scope or be it making changes in people who are allocated to perform the work.

- The composition change in the Development Team can happen between two Sprints. The Development Team is self-organizing, but it does not mean that they can change their composition mid-Sprint.

- Inside the Sprint time-box, the team is expected to work at a sustainable pace to complete a chosen set of work that aligns with a Sprint Goal.

- Time-boxing limits the work in process items, as the team plans to work on only those items that it believes it can start and finish within the Sprint.

- Time-boxing improves predictability, as it is reasonable to expect that we can predict the work we can complete in the next short Sprint as compared to long-duration deliveries.

- The team does not have to be locked away in a container for too long, which risk them losing a grip on the changing world.

Benefits of Short Duration Sprint

- Early Feedback

- Early Return on Investment

- We go wrong in a small way as Sprint duration is short

- Regular inspections at the end of each short Sprint

Sprint Length

- Sprints should be consistent in length as fixed Sprint length benefits the Scrum teams, though exceptions are permitted under certain circumstances.

- If Sprint lengths are consistent, then you can schedule the Sprint Planning, Sprint Review, and Sprint Retrospective activities for many Sprints in one go otherwise extra efforts are needed to coordinate the schedules with all stakeholders.

- Sprint time-box should never be extended to complete the remaining work.

When and Who Defines the Sprint Length?

The Scrum Team should discuss and come up about the first Sprint length before starting the Sprint. The length of the following Sprints can be changed. There is no formal event for this purpose. Following points can be taken into account:

- Changing market conditions and the frequency at which the requirements change.

- The level of uncertainty about the technology.

- How often the Scrum team needs feedback from the Product Owner and customers.

- The duration for which the Scrum team can stay focused on the goal, the teams' maturity, its product knowledge, and the interdependencies with external teams.

- The pace at which the Product Owner wants to have increments (new features implemented), demonstrate them to the Key Stakeholders, and get feedback.

- Experience of the Development Team. Too long Sprints make planning challenging. Too short Sprints do not allow implementing bigger features in one chunk but giving faster feedback.

Cancelling a Sprint

A Sprint will be canceled if the Sprint Goal becomes obsolete. This might occur if the company changes direction or if the market or technology conditions change.

A Sprint can be canceled before the Sprint time-box is over. Only the Product Owner has the authority to cancel the Sprint, although he or she may do so under influence from the stakeholders, the Development Team, or the Scrum Master.

In general, a Sprint should be canceled if it no longer makes sense given the circumstances. Due to the short duration of Sprints, cancellation rarely makes sense.

When a Sprint is canceled:

- Any completed and Done Product Backlog Items are reviewed.

- If part of the work is potentially releasable, the Product Owner typically accepts it.

- All incomplete Product Backlog Items are re-estimated and put back on the Product Backlog. The work done on them depreciates quickly and must be frequently re-estimated.

Sprint cancellations consume resources since everyone regroups in another Sprint Planning to start another Sprint. Sprint cancellations are often traumatic to the Scrum Team and are very uncommon.

A Development Team should not seek an unrealistic goal as there is a high risk of wasted effort.

The remaining days/time of a canceled Sprint time-box should be used to plan and achieve a more realistic Goal. The team should try to extract as much value out of work done as possible. The problems that have occurred must be addressed and resolved in the Sprint Retrospective, as the agreement of an unattainable Goal represents a severe material defect in the application of Scrum.

Sample Questions

Q: From the first Sprint, the Scrum team starts interacting with each other, and as everyone is new, they start spending time getting to know each other on the Scrum Team. Hence, except the first Sprint, the product should always be in a potentially releasable condition at the end of the Sprint. True or False.

Q: The amount of uncertainty about the technology to be used is also taken into account when determining the length of the Sprint. True or False.

Q: Help yourself in finding out what needs to be in place before first Sprint starts? Select all applicable

1. A complete Product Backlog of requirements.
2. Just enough Product Backlog Items for the first Sprint.
3. Architecture must be completed so that Development can start from first Sprint.
4. Architecture must be determined and documented so that Development can start from first Sprint.
5. A complete Sprint Backlog of requirements.

Q: Architecture can be discussed during Product Backlog Refinement and is developed along with selected Product Backlog Items. True or False.

Q: What are the ways in which Scrum handles architecture and infrastructure?

1. Architecture and infrastructure requirements are added in the Product Backlog as Product Backlog Items and are addressed in early Sprints.
2. They must be addressed and completed before first Sprint.
3. They must be determined and documented before first Sprint so that Development can start from first Sprint.
4. Add them to the definition of Done.

Q: Scrum does not mention any specific upper limit for Development Team size. True or False

Q: The risk of being disconnected from the stakeholders is also considered when determining the Sprint duration. True or False.

Q: What are the in which Scrum team handles security and safety requirements?

1. Security and Safety department should take care of this work.
2. Add security and safety requirements to the definition of Done.
3. Add security and safety requirements to the Product Backlog.
4. Scrum Master takes care of security and safety requirements.

Q: Help yourself in finding the factors that are considered when determining the Sprint duration? Select all applicable

1. Development Team size.
2. The organization's policy for length of the Sprints. If organization do not have any standard policy then team can go ahead with standard two weeks Sprint.
3. The capacity to go to market with a product release.
4. Scrum Master's availability for the Sprint duration.

Q: Inspection is done at any time during a Sprint, but adaption should done from the next Sprint onwards, as interruption in Sprint may reduce the velocity of the Development Team. True or False

Q: Scrum Master can cancel a Sprint. True or False

Q: If all Product Backlog Items selected during the Sprint Planning meeting are done before the Sprint duration expiry, the Sprint can be considered over. True or False

Q: The Product Backlog Items selected during the Sprint Planning meeting can be re-negotiated during the Sprint. True or False

Q: Scrum does not advise Development Teams with more than nine developers because

1. Daily Scrum time-box is 15 minutes; if team size is more than 9 then Daily Scrum meetings cannot be finished in 15 minutes.
2. It becomes difficult for the Product Owner to assign the Sprint Backlog Items.
3. Too much complexity is generated.
4. Scrum does advise Development Teams with more than nine developers.

Q: During the Sprint, changes should be made even if that may endanger the Sprint Goal. True or False

Q: A new developer Sindhu asked another developer Jeff, when could Sprint be abnormally canceled. Select all applicable

1. Half of the Development Team is on vacation.
2. The Development Team feels that complexity of task is too high compared to what they initially predicted.
3. Product is going on vacation for entire Sprint duration
4. When the Sprint Goal becomes obsolete

Q: All the Scrum Teams working on the same Product should have the same Sprint length. True or False.

Q: During the Sprint, no changes are made that would endanger the Sprint Goal. True or False

Q: What are the benefits of keeping the Sprint duration consistent throughout the project? Select all applicable

1. It is a waste of time in defining the Sprint duration repeatedly. Hence keeping the same Sprint duration, saves the time spent of redefining the Sprint duration
2. Developers are more happy and satisfied when Sprint duration is consistent
3. It offers a consistent mechanism of measuring team velocity
4. All of the above

Q: With consistent Sprint length throughout the Sprint, a consistent delivery pattern can be established. True or False

Q: All Scrum teams working on the same product should begin and end Sprint at the same time. True or False.

Q: Lionel a new developer just joined a Scrum team. He wanted to know what should be done when a new requirement arises while a Scrum project is running. What do you think?

1. Scrum is created for adopting changes hence new requirements should be included in the project automatically.
2. Requirements should be considered for next Sprint.
3. Requirements are evaluated for significance and are included in the project if they are relevant to the business.
4. Scrum Master is responsible for deciding the requirement change requests.

Q: The Development Team's composition stays constant throughout Sprints. Do you agree? Yes or No

Q: A new Product Owner Ajara was discussing in a Scrum session that if User Stories can be changed or not at any time during the Sprint. Scrum Master Stacy shared some reason why Scrum prevents Product Owners from altering User Stories during the Sprint. Help yourself to identify those reasons. Select all applicable

1. Developers cannot complete their committed Product Backlog Items if requirements are changing during Sprint execution
2. Avoid conflict between Scrum Master and Product Owner on changing the requirements
3. This helps Product Owners to concentrate on what is most important for the Development Team to develop
4. As Sprint length is fixed, User Stories should also be fixed during Sprint execution

Q: During the Sprint, the scope should not be re-negotiated between the Product Owner and Development Team as scope finalization is already done in Sprint Planning meeting. True or False

Q: One of the Development Team member Melissa identified one technical issue of web page loading time. The Development Team decides to work together to solve loading time issue. Who needs to facilitate the discussion among Development Team members?

1. Scrum Master
2. Development Team
3. Load Test Engineer
4. Product Owner

Q: Consistent Sprint length throughout the project helps in the following.

1. Easy planning and forecasting the work
2. To minimize the risk and delay
3. Scrum Master can be shared across multiple projects
4. All of the above

Q: In a startup organization Mayakovskaya Corp, a Scrum project is started. Development team size is 7 and a Scrum Master Shakira and Product Owner Adele is working on two weeks Sprint. In one of the Sprint, after one week 60% of work was in progress. The Development Team decided to divide the remaining Sprint Backlog Items and assigns ownership of every Sprint Backlog Item to individual developers in the team to expedite the development. What will Shakira do?

1. Shakira discuss with Adele and then agrees with team's decision; she feels it will help to complete more work (60 %).
2. Shakira discuss with Adele and then agrees with team's decision; she feels it will increase utilization of every developer and increases individual accountability.

3. Shakira disagrees with that. She coaches the Development Team to jointly take ownership of Sprint Backlog Items.

4. Shakira agrees with that. She inform the Development Team that they are finally responsible for the product delivery.

Q: Junior developer Kavya said, during the Sprint the scope might be clarified and re-negotiated between the Product Owner and Development Team as more is learned. Do you agree with Kavya? True or False

Q: Scrum does not stop to have a 'Hardening' Sprint to remove all technical debt so that Product Increment can be developed in an upcoming release. True or False

Q: Scrum does not stop to have a 'Zero' Sprint to remove all technical debt so that Product Increment can be developed in an upcoming release. True or False

Q: Which of the following must be delivered at the end of a Sprint. Select all applicable

1. A user manual that helps end users to use the Product Increment.

2. A Scrum Guide that helps end users to adapt the Scrum.

3. An Increment of working software that is Done.

4. An Increment of working software that is Done and few Undone Product Backlog Items.

Q: Development Team can deliver a single document if Product Owner ask for that document at the end of a Sprint. Do you agree with this? True or False.

Q: A new developer Freddie, was not sure on how frequently Scrum artifacts needs to be revived. In one Scrum session, he asked this question to Scrum Master, Connie. Help yourself to select Connie's reply from following. Select all applicable.

1. Immediately after the Daily Scrum

2. Frequently, but it should not get in the way of the work

3. At the Sprint Review

4. At the Sprint Retrospective

Q: Development Team must make adjustments to its engineering practices before a Sprint begins? True or False

Q: In a Scrum team of two weeks Sprints, first Sprint is going to complete in 5 days. Scrum Master, Zhang is planning to send a meeting invite for the Sprint Review. It is expected to demo the items completed in the Sprint. Whom should Zhang invite as a required attendee?

1. Product Owner

2. Development Team

3. Business Users

4. All of the above

5. Product Owner & Development Team

Q: In a Sprint Planning, Development Team is pulling the work into the Sprint from the actual Product Backlog. The team is selecting the amount of work it deems feasible for the Sprint considering the Definition of Done and the average work completed in previous Sprints. Development Team has found that work pulled has grown beyond their capacity. What should Development Team do? Select all applicable

1. Do Nothing. All incomplete Sprint Backlog Items will be pushed back to Product Backlog during Sprint Review

2. Collaborate with the Product Owner and possibly remove or modify Sprint Backlog Items

3. Add additional developers to complete all selected items.

4. Extend Sprint's length only for the current Sprint s that they can deliver as committed

Q: The Scrum team decides Sprint length by dividing the total number of story points by the average velocity of the team. True of False.

Q: A new developer, Lindsay is eager to know when will she become the sole owner of a Sprint Backlog Item. She asks this question to Scrum Master Katie. Help yourself in selecting the answer of Katie from the following.

1. At the Sprint Planning meeting when all developers self-assign the tasks for themselves.
2. Never. All Sprint Backlog Items are "owned" by the entire Development Team.
3. If Lindsay implements the item entirely from end to end (front end to backend), she will become the sole owner of that item.
4. Both 1 & 3

Q: Multiple Scrum teams working on the same Product must have the same Sprint start date. True or False?

Q: In the middle of a Sprint, the key stakeholder Dara decides that two new features she want on priority which are not considered in current Sprint. What should Product Owner Maria do? Select two

1. Maria asks the Development Team to check if it is possible for them to add these features in the current Sprint
2. The Scrum Master add these features to the current Sprint
3. Maria adds the new features to Product Backlog
4. Maria adds the new features to Sprint Backlog
5. Maria adds the new features to Product Backlog and Sprint Backlog if Development Team says they can complete these additional features in same Sprint

Q: A new Product Owner, Janet wants to know what all activities she can do during a Sprint.

1. Answer the Development Team's questions about the current Sprint Items as needed
2. Attend the Daily Scrum to listen and resolve the Development Team's obstacles

3. Work with the stakeholder for product features

4. All of the above

Q: Development Team must make adjustments to its engineering practices before starting a project? True or False

Q: When does fresh work or further sub tasks are added to the Sprint Backlog during a Sprint?

1. When new features are identified by the Product Owner.

2. After they have been identified as quickly as possible.

3. As soon as possible after they are approved by Scrum Master.

4. If technical debt starts increasing, it should be added immediately.

Q: If a Sprint Backlog Item is not finished by the end of the Sprint, the Sprint should be canceled. True or False

Q: Who has the authority to cancel the Sprint?

1. The Development Team

2. The Scrum Master

3. Scrum Team

4. The Product Owner

Q: What happens when a Sprint is canceled? Select all applicable

1. Development Team keeps on working till Sprint duration expiry. They may use this period to reduce the technical debt reduction.

2. Any Product Backlog Items completed and Done are reviewed.

3. If portion of the work can be released, it is typically accepted by the Product Owner.

4. In a Sprint Cancelation meeting, detailed status report must be created in which cause of Sprint cancelation must be added and shared with all stakeholders.

Q: When is a Sprint over?

1. When all the tasks are completed. Development Team should start the next Sprint immediately without waiting for complete Sprint duration.
2. When the Product Owner and Scrum Master declares it is done.
3. When the time-box expires.
4. When the time-box expires or there are no further tasks in Sprint Backlog.
5. All of the above

Q: The purpose of a Sprint is to produce a done increment of a working shippable product. True or False

Q: Which of the following does the Development Team do during the first Sprint? Select all applicable

1. Define the complete architecture for the product. Without complete architecture in place, developers will not be able to develop quality code in subsequent Sprints.
2. Build the whole Product Backlog to be developed in subsequent Sprints.
3. Develop and deliver at least one piece of functionality.
4. Assign the roles and responsibilities of all developers so that there will not be any conflict in subsequent Sprints.

Q: When will the next Sprint start? Select all applicable

1. Immediately after the Sprint Review of the previous Sprint.
2. Immediately after the conclusion of the previous Sprint.
3. When the Product Owner is ready for discussion on Product Backlog Items so that Development Team can create their Sprint Backlog.
4. Immediate next working day after the completion of the previous Sprint.

Q: In a startup organization, a new Scrum Team has started adopting the Scrum. In a Scrum training, one developer Gabrielle asked how much work Development Team must do with respect to selected Product Backlog Item for a Sprint. What will you reply to Gabrielle?

1. Everything assigned in Sprint Backlog by Scrum Master to every developer.
2. Everything discussed in Daily Scrum and that can fit into the Sprint.
3. Analysis, design, programming, testing, and documentation.
4. As much as Product Owner has asked Development Team to do for every selected Product Backlog Item in accordance with the definition of Done.
5. Both 2 & 3
6. None of the above.

Q: Anthoine, a junior developer wanted to know about any guideline on changing Developer in Development Team. When should Developer be changed in Development Team? Help yourself to answer Anthoine. Select all applicable

1. After every six month as rotating the developers is very important
2. It should never be changed unless developer resign or ask for release from the project.
3. As needed, while taking into account a short-term reduction in productivity.
4. As needed, with there will not be any impact on productivity.

Q: It is not mandatory that the working Product Increment must be released to production at the end of each Sprint. True or False

Q: Jackie, a developer new to Scrum wanted to know about any guideline on what happens when all selected Product Backlog Items are not completed at the end of the Sprint. What will you suggest to Jackie?

1. Extend the Sprint duration as there is no point in delivering the increment with incomplete features
2. Incomplete items are returned back to the Product Backlog
3. Mark incomplete PBIs for next Sprint
4. Product Owner is responsible to deciding on what action needs to be taken on incomplete items

Q: During a Sprint, a Development Team of 7 members finds that they will not be able to finish the selected user stories. Selected stories and work required in that Sprint should be reviewed. What do you think who all should be present to discuss and adjust the Sprint work selected?

1. The Scrum Master, Technical Experts and the Development Team.
2. The Product Owner and the Development Team.
3. The Product Owner and all stakeholders.
4. The Product Owner and the developers who are working on the user stories which they are not able to finish on time.
5. The Development Team.

Q: Two new developers Joshua and Elon were debating on if subsequent Sprints always starts after completion of previous Sprint. Joshua was saying Product Owner may postpone the start of a new Sprint after the completion of an ongoing Sprint in some of the scenarios. Elon was not agreeing with Joshua. What are your views on postponing the subsequent Sprints in some scenarios? Select all applicable.

1. All Sprint Backlog Items in current Sprint is not completed hence current Sprint should be extended and new Sprint will postpone even after current Sprint's expiry.
2. Product Backlog Items for subsequent Sprints are not in "Ready" state.

3. As per Elon, a new Sprint begins immediately after the completion of the previous Sprint; there are no acceptable reasons to postpone it.

4. Scrum Master may decide to postpone next Sprint if more than 50% of Development Team members are on vacations.

Q: The Scrum team decides Sprint length based on the size and complexity of the project. True of False.

Q: Who decides the duration of the Sprint?

1. Sprint Manager
2. Scrum Master
3. Development Team
4. Product Owner and Scrum Master
5. Scrum Team

Q: A junior developer, Warren wanted to know about what happens to a Sprint Backlog Item that was not completed until Sprint ends. What would you suggest to Warren? Select all applicable

1. As selected items was of top priority hence was selected for implementation, if it is not completed in current Sprint, it should be completed in the next Sprint
2. It will be demonstrated to the stakeholders in Sprint Review meeting and will be informed that that it is in progress
3. The Sprint should be extended till the item is completed
4. None of the above

Q: Scrum employs time-boxing to prevent occurrences from exceeding a predetermined time box. True or False

Q: Scrum framework ensures Product Owner is not interrupted by developers during the Sprint. True or False.

Q: When does the next Sprint starts? Select all applicable

1. After the working Product Increment is released to production.
2. If Sprint Review is on Friday, next Sprint starts on Monday
3. Next working day, after completing the Sprint Retrospective event of the current Sprint.
4. None of the above.

Chapter 8

Scrum Process Flow

Sprint Planning

Overview

A release can have one or more Sprints. Every Sprint begins with Sprint Planning. Scrum team performs Sprint Planning to determine the most important subset of Product Backlog Items to build in the Sprint. Development Team pulls work into the Sprint from the actual Product Backlog.

Sprint Planning is time-boxed to a maximum of eight hours for a one-month Sprint. For shorter Sprints, the event is usually shorter.

The work to be performed in the Sprint is planned at the Sprint Planning. This plan is created by the collaborative work of the entire Scrum Team. The team selects the amount of work it deems feasible (it is a forecast, not a commitment) for the Sprint considering the Definition of Done and the average work completed in previous Sprints.

The Scrum Master ensures that the event takes place and that attendants understand its purpose. The Scrum Master teaches the Scrum Team to keep it within the time-box.

Scrum Master observes the planning activity, ask probing questions, and facilitates to help ensure a successful result. Scrum Master generally facilitates the meeting. However, others in the Scrum team may also facilitate the meeting, if required.

Sprint Planning answers the following:

- What can be delivered in the Increment resulting from the upcoming Sprint?

- How will the work needed to deliver the Increment be achieved?

Inputs

The input to this meeting is:

- The Product Backlog

- The latest product Increment

- The projected capacity of the Development Team

- Past performance of the Development Team

- Definition of Done

- Constraints & Impediments

- Retrospective improvements from previous Sprint

What Can be Done in the Sprint

The Development Team works to forecast the functionality that is developed during the Sprint. The Product Owner discusses the objective that the Sprint should achieve and the Product Backlog Items that, if completed in the Sprint, would achieve the Sprint Goal. The entire Scrum Team collaborates on understanding the work of the Sprint. Architecture and design emerge across multiple Sprints, rather than being developed entirely during the first Sprints.

The number of items selected from the Product Backlog for the Sprint is solely up to the Development Team. Only the Development Team can assess what it can accomplish over the upcoming Sprint. The views of the Product Owner are respected, and additionally, details are discussed with the Product Owner during this meeting.

During Sprint Planning, the Scrum Team crafts a Sprint Goal. The Sprint Goal is an objective that is met within the Sprint through the implementation of the Product Backlog, and it guides the Development Team on why it is building the Increment.

Sprint Capacity

A Scrum team should define and declare its capacity before kick-starting the work forecasted for the Sprint. It avoids delays in reaching the Sprint Goal.

- In a two-week Sprint, the team does not have ten days (five working days in a week) as team capacity for Sprint execution.

- Roughly, one and a half-day of time is needed collectively for Sprint events - Sprint Planning, Daily Scrum, Sprint Review, and Sprint Retrospective.

- Product backlog grooming should not exceed 10% of the team's available capacity

- The team should consider the time needed for other non-Sprint activities like support, maintenance, working on other projects, and so on.

- The team should consider the time needed for reading and writing the emails, attending the HR sessions, fire drills, and so on.

- Consider team members leaves during Sprint.

- Reserve some buffer against unexpected problems. How much should be the buffer time? The team can find out the best number after completing a few Sprints.

- Team capacity should not include the time spent on Scrum events, backlog grooming, organization-level activities, leaves, and buffer.

- The unit for capacity could be story points, ideal days, or the hours.

- The team should consider predicted velocity and the available capacity for selecting the Product Backlog Items for a Sprint during the planning

Example:

Table 5: Determining capacity in hours

Team member	Total days	Leaves (days)	Other Scrum activities (days)	Hours per day (hours)	Available hours
TM1	10	0	2.5	4–7	30–52.5
TM2	10	0	2.5	5–6	37.5–45
TM3	10	2	2.5	4–6	22–33
TM4	10	2	2.5	2–3	11–16.5
Total					100.5–147

The capacity calculation is done as follows:

- The team members find out how many days they are available for work.

- Member 3 & 4 is planning for two-day leaves.

- For other Scrum activities, 2.5 days are considered.

- Team members consider the time required for non-Sprint activities and organizational level activities.

- Member 4 is half time on the project. Hence half time needs to be considered.

- Each team member determines how many hours per day they could dedicate to work in this Sprint.

- In this example, a total capacity of 100.5–147 hours is estimated.

How Will the Chosen Work Get Done

Having set the Sprint Goal and selected the Product Backlog Items for the Sprint, the Development Team decides how it will build this functionality into a Done Product Increment during the Sprint. The Product Backlog Items selected for this Sprint plus the plan for delivering them (list of actionable development work) is called the Sprint Backlog.

The Development Team usually starts by designing & analyzing the system and the work needed (list of actionable development work) to convert the Product Backlog into a working product Increment. Work may be of varying size, or estimated effort. However, enough work is planned during Sprint Planning for the Development Team to forecast what it believes it can do in the upcoming Sprint.

Work planned for the first days of the Sprint by the Development Team is decomposed to tasks by the end of this meeting, often to units of one day or less. All Product Backlog Items are not required to be decomposed to tasks or needs to be understood completely in Sprint Planning meeting. It is an ongoing process. The team must take care though that at least some of the PBIs are completely understood and decomposed into tasks so that the team has work for at least the first couple of days. The rest of the PBIs can be detailed as an ongoing process throughout the Sprint.

The Development Team self-organizes to undertake the work in the Sprint Backlog, both during Sprint Planning and as needed throughout the Sprint.

The Product Owner can help to clarify the selected Product Backlog Items and make trade-offs. If the Development Team determines it has too much or too little work, it may renegotiate the selected Product Backlog Items with the Product Owner.

The Development Team may also invite other people to attend to provide technical or domain advice.

By the end of the Sprint Planning, the Development Team should be able to explain to the Product Owner and Scrum Master how it intends to work as a self-organizing team to accomplish the Sprint Goal and create the anticipated Increment.

Participants

- All the members of the Scrum Team should participate in the Sprint Planning.

- The Development Team may invite technical or domain experts external to the team to provide any required input or guidance.

Sprint Planning Outputs

- Sprint Goal

- Sprint Backlog

Sprint Goal

The Sprint Goal is an objective set for the Sprint that can be met through the implementation of Product Backlog. It provides guidance to the Development Team on why it is building the Increment. It is created during the Sprint Planning meeting. Sprint Goals should be specific and measurable.

The Sprint Goal gives the Development Team some flexibility regarding the functionality implemented within the Sprint. The selected Product Backlog Items deliver one coherent function, which can be the Sprint Goal. The Sprint Goal can be any other coherence that causes the Development Team to work together rather than on separate initiatives.

During the Sprint, no changes are made that would put the Sprint Goal at risk. If Sprint Goal does not seem achievable, the Development Team has the courage to tell the Product Owner. They collaborate with the Product Owner to negotiate the scope of Sprint Backlog within the Sprint. The Product Owner respects the Development Team's opinion on whether they can achieve it.

As the Development Team works, it keeps the Sprint Goal in mind. In order to satisfy the Sprint Goal, it implements functionality and technology. While the selected work for the Sprint Backlog represents a forecast, the Development Team gives its commitment to achieving the Sprint Goal.

Some examples of Sprint Goal:

- Support the application on Internet Explorer in addition to the Chrome browser.

- Improve the performance of the application by 20 percentage.

- We create some tangible functionality, to show the organization that we can deliver software using Scrum

- We fix the major bugs that users have reported to be the biggest problem in our product.

How to Choose a Sprint Goal

To determine what the Sprint Goal should be, consider following questions:

- Why do we carry out the Sprint?

- What should be achieved in the Sprint?

- How do we reach its goal?

- How do we know the goal has been met?

Where Can We Write Sprint Goal?

Sprint Backlog and Sprint Goal both are created during the Sprint Planning meeting. The Sprint Backlog is the set of Product Backlog Items selected for the Sprint, plus a plan for delivering the product Increment and realizing the Sprint Goal. So do we write Sprint Goal in the Sprint Backlog? The answer is NO. Sprint Backlog is there to support the attainment of a Sprint Goal and not the other way around.

Some teams write the Sprint Goal above their Scrum Boards. Scrum does not prescribe where to write the goal. However, it should be visible to the Scrum team and all stakeholders.

Sprint Execution

Overview

Sprint Execution is not an event. Sprint Execution time is the period between Sprint Planning and the Sprint Review. In this period, the Scrum team carries out the work to meet the goal and produces the potentially shippable Product Increment. In this period, the team also perform activities like Sprint Review preparation, Product Backlog Refinement, and so on.

Participants

- Development Team members - Development team, identify when and who should do the work, any task level dependencies, and the order of the tasks. The Development Team executes the tasks without blocking any other tasks. Team members work on an item to finish what has already been started before moving ahead to start work on new items. The goal is to maximize the total value delivered during the Sprint i.e., the total number of items Done during the Sprint.

- The Scrum Master - Scrum Master, help everyone understand the Scrum. Scrum Master collaborates with Product Owner, Development Team, and outsiders to the Scrum Team. Scrum Master is a coach to the Development Team and PO.

- The Product Owner - Product Owner answer the queries of the Development Team members on Product Backlog Items during the Sprint execution.

Inputs

- Sprint Goal

- Sprint Backlog

Outputs

- Potentially shippable Product Increment

Scrum Board

Scrum board is used to communicate Scrum Team's progress. Table 6 depicts a typical Scrum board with tasks being measured in hours; the team may choose to put other columns as needed.

Table 6: A typical Scrum Board

PBIs	Task not started	Work in progress	Blocked	Completed
PBI 1	Task 3, Hours = 2 Task 4, Hours = 3	Task 2, Hours = 4		Task 1, Hours = 4
PBI 2	Task 2, Task 3		Task 1	
PBI 3	Task 2, Task 3			Task 1
PBI 4	Task 1, Task 2			
PBI 5	Task 1, Task 2, Task 3			

Product Backlog Items, along with their planned tasks, are shown on the Scrum Board. All tasks are initially kept in 'Task not started' column. Development Team members start selecting the tasks from 'Task not started' column and move them into the 'Work in progress' column. Completed tasks are moved to the 'Completed' column. If any Development Team member is struggling for completing the task and support is needed for completing it, he or she should show the courage value to inform task status as blocked and ask for help from others. They should be moved to the 'Blocked' column.

Sprint Burndown Chart

Sprint Burndown Chart shows the amount of work remaining (estimated efforts) during a Sprint. Let us consider an example to understand the Sprint Burndown Chart. One Scrum Team is following two weeks Sprint and Development Team members efforts for completing the tasks are in hours. Day by day as Sprint progresses Development Team members update their efforts each day.

Table 7: Tasks with hours remaining day by day

Tasks	Day1	Day2	Day3	Day4	Day5	...	Day10
Task 1	10	4	4	2			
Task 2	14	14	10	12	8		
Task 3	7	7	7	7	7		
Task 4			14	9			
Task 5–20	120	115	110	100	90		
Total	150	140	145	130	105		0

Table 7 shows tasks with hours remaining to complete the work.

Task 1. On day 2 and day 3, hours remaining are the same. The reason could be that the developer has not worked on this task or developer worked and new work added with more clarity on the task.

Task 2. The developer discussed with the Product Owner for more clarity of the work. As more efforts are needed than estimated earlier, on day 4 developer updated efforts remaining as 12.

Task 3. It is not started. Hence it is showing the same efforts every day.

Task 4. A new task is added on day 3.

If we plot the total sum of the remaining effort hours across all uncompleted tasks on a given day, on a graph, we get the Sprint burndown chart. You can draw a simple XY axis graph. The X-axis is days within a Sprint – D1, D2, D3...D10, Y-axis is estimated hours remaining – 150,140,145,130,105...0

Sprint Burnup Chart

Sprint burnup chart represents the amount of work (usually story points or ideal days) completed in a Sprint. Many teams use burnup charts to know the business valuable work completed during the Sprint

You can draw a simple XY axis graph. X-axis is days within a Sprint – D1, D2, D3...D10, Y-axis is story points completed during Sprint – 0,10,20,30,40..110

Daily Scrum

Overview

Daily Scrum is a formal opportunity for the Development Team to inspect and adapt its progress towards the Sprint Goal. The Daily Scrum event is a 15-minute time-boxed meeting. If the Development Team finishes the daily scum, they can end it with less than 15 minutes.

The Daily Scrum is held every day of the Sprint. At it, the Development Team plans work for the next 24 hours. This optimizes team collaboration and performance by inspecting the work since the last Daily Scrum and forecasting upcoming Sprint work. The Development Team holds this meeting to manage and follow up on its development work. When Development Team members miss the Daily Scrum meeting, they miss an opportunity to inspect and adapt, also get out of sync with the rest of the team.

Daily Scrum is not a traditional status meeting. However, it can be useful to communicate the status of Sprint Backlog Items among the Development Team members. Daily Scrum identifies the impediments that prevent the progress of the Development Team's work, though Daily Scrum is not a problem-solving activity. The Development Team or interested team members often meet immediately after the Daily Scrum for detailed discussions, to talk about problems, or to adapt, or re-plan, the rest of the Sprint's work.

The Development Team uses the Daily Scrum to inspect progress toward the Sprint Goal and to inspect how progress is trending toward completing the work in the Sprint Backlog. Adaption is captured in an update of the Sprint Backlog. The Daily Scrum optimizes the probability that the Development Team meets the Sprint Goal. If the actual progress impacts upon the forecast or Development Team discovers that they have overcommitted for the Sprint, the Development Team consults with the Product Owner to adjust the Sprint scope. Every day, the Development Team should understand how it intends to work together as a self-organizing team to accomplish the Sprint Goal and create the anticipated Increment by the end of the Sprint.

The structure of the meeting is set by the Development Team and can be conducted in different ways if it focuses on progress toward the Sprint Goal. Some Development Teams use questions, and some make it more discussion-based. Here is an example of what might be used:

- What did I do yesterday that helped the Development Team meet the Sprint Goal?

- What will I do today to help the Development Team meet the Sprint Goal?

- Do I see any impediment that prevents me or the Development Team from meeting the Sprint Goal?

It is a myth that everyone has to follow this approach of answering the above three questions. The Development Team can decide the format suitable for them.

The Daily Scrum is held at the same time and place each day to reduce complexity. It sets a routine that makes it easier for people to follow. The Scrum Master ensures that the Development Team has the meeting, but the Development Team is responsible for conducting the Daily Scrum.

The Scrum Master teaches the Development Team to keep the Daily Scrum within the 15-minute time-box. Time-box is 15-minutes irrespective of the size of the Development Team and the length of the Sprint.

The Daily Scrum is an internal meeting for the Development Team. The Scrum Master enforces the rule that only the Development Team participates. If others are present, the Scrum Master ensures that they do not disrupt the meeting.

Daily Scrums:

- Improve communications

- Eliminate other meetings

- Identify impediments to development for removal

- Highlight and promote quick decision-making

- Improve the Development Team's level of knowledge.

This is a key inspect and adapt meeting.

Participants

- It is mandatory for all the Development Team members to attend the Daily Scrum. Participants of Daily Scrum are Development team members.

- Product Owner is the optional attendee. If PO attends the Daily Scrum - PO is generally a silent observer, may speak at the request of the Development team for any clarifications in the forecasted Sprint Goal. PO may bring to the notice of the team members any new developments that might impact the Sprint Goal. PO may use the Daily Scrum as an opportunity to cancel the Sprint if the Sprint Goal has been come obsolete.

- Scrum Master is the optional attendee. SM may attend the Daily Scrum if the Development Team is new to the Scrum framework to ensure Daily Scrums are effective, are self-organized, and add value. Scrum Master may initially need to help facilitate the Daily Scrum for the Development Team until they are able to conduct it themselves.

- If others (who are not the part of the Development Team) are present, the Scrum Master ensures that they do not disrupt the meeting. The Scrum Values include Focus and Respect. When the Development Team seek focus, this must be respected.

Inputs

Inputs to the Daily Scrum are:

- Every Development Team member would bring the information on the work performed since the last Daily Scrum
- Sprint Backlog
- Sprint Goal
- List of impediments

Outputs

Outputs of the Daily Scrum are:

- Updated Sprint Backlog
- Updated Sprint Goal (if the earlier goal becomes obsolete)
- Updated list of impediments

Recommendations

10 tips to improve your Daily Scrum by Scott Oliver are:

1. Stick to the 15 minutes time-box - If your Daily Scrum is running over then it may be time to look at what is going on within it. It is not easy to interrupt someone talking, but if

they are rambling and not adding value, do not be afraid to jump in. There is plenty time outside of the Daily Scrum to have bigger conversations. Let us try keep the Daily Scrum focused and stick to the time-box.

2. What are you saying? - The Daily Scrum is a chance for the team to inspect their progress towards the Sprint Goal. The Development Team should be using their skills, knowledge and experience to plan how they are going to continue progress towards the Sprint Goal. This may be as simple as a developer asking for help on a specific issue for example "Pair with me so we can get the work done". Or it could be a developer holding someone else accountable, asking why they are working on something new when their previous work is still in progress. The team should keep focus and avoid turning the conversations into status updates and rambling on about non-related things. They should avoid getting too technical as that could be discussed outside the Daily Scrum. Each time a person speaks, they should be adding value.

3. To three questions or not to three questions - The Development Team must decide how they want to organize this event. Some teams will use a predetermined set of questions each team member's answers, but this is not prescribed. In many teams, developers may be asking questions like: Can I help you with this task? ,Who can help me with this task?, Can you tell me what you think about this?, How shall we approach this together? It is good to mix things up from time to time, change up how the team are conducting the Daily Scrum. One way is to have the person who speaks next, start their first sentence with the last word the previous person used. Or how about asking everyone to close their eyes during the Daily Scrum? Maybe tell the team they cannot show their teeth during the entire meeting? I realize these are corny, but give them a try and see what the outcome is.

4. Project managers are here! - The Daily Scrum is an internal meeting for the Development Team. This means that anyone outside of the Development Team that are present should not be disrupting it. The Scrum Master should also ensure others do not disrupt things too. Without this level of protection or willingness to challenge. We run the risk of the Daily Scrum falling into a status update. This is a major factor in people starting to devalue the Daily Scrum. I prefer it if it is only the Scrum team that is present. This includes the Product Owner. It is always good to have that transparency across the whole Scrum team.

5. What time do we have it? - There is no prescribed time to have the Daily Scrum, as long as it is held at the same time and same place each day to reduce complexity. The specific time can be whatever the team are comfortable with. If the idea is to inspect, plan and adapt for the next 24 hours then I find it is better to hold the Daily Scrum as soon as possible. In my experience if you are running the Daily Scrum at 11am or 1pm then it's not going to have the same impact. The working day is already underway and conversations will have already been held. I recommend asking the team what time they are all going to be present and then agree a time that suits everyone.

6. Does the Scrum Master facilitate it? - A lot of people think that the Scrum Master must facilitate the Daily Scrum. However, this is not true, if the Development Team ask the Scrum Master to facilitate then the Scrum Master can. However as mentioned before, this is a meeting for the Development Team. If we look at self-organizing teams, they don't need someone directing them and telling them what to do. If the team rely on a Scrum Master to facilitate the Daily Scrum. They would become dependent on that person. By allowing the Scrum Master to facilitate, it removes the empowerment and self-organizing element. The reliance on the Scrum Master will

cause issues and it will end up being more of a meeting rather than a valuable Scrum Event.

7. Let us hold each other accountable – Developers should not be afraid to challenge each other, to have a voice and hold each other accountable. We should be encouraging a no-blame culture, where we look to fail fast and learn from our failures only to improve going forward. Do not be afraid to challenge other members of the team during the Daily Scrum. Having physical boards is great. Making visible the work helps the team hold each other accountable. For example if a team member is discussing work they are working on and it is sitting in the 'To do' column on the board. The accountability is already there for that person, it is obvious and the team will know it.

8. Who speaks and when? - A difficult one for newer Scrum teams. Nobody willing to talk or take that first step. Or others chatting amongst themselves when someone else is talking. The Daily Scrum should keep focus and it is a great chance to inspect and adapt. Those present should listen to the person talking and respond only when required. One tip is to use a talking ball, this can be any object that is used to symbolize when someone is speaking. If you have the talking ball, you speak, if you have not, you listen. One person speaks at a time. I start by passing the ball to someone, signaling the start. Then they choose whom they pass the ball to next. There is accountability too, if you drop the ball because you were not paying attention, it will be obvious to everyone. Nobody wants to be that person.

9. Stand-up, sit down and location – It is a common practice of everyone standing up during the meeting to ensure that the meeting does not go on forever. However, it is not mandatory to stand up. It is a myth that everyone has to standup. Standing up usually helps the team keep focus and also keep it

within the time-box. You do not want to be standing up for a long time. If you are all co-located, get together and face each other around your Scrum Board. Nothing beats face-to-face communication. Not only will it be easier to understand each other and respond. You can also get a feel for body language and tone of voice easier.

10. Be prepared ahead of time - Before you attend the Daily Scrum, I like people to be prepared. If you are not prepared for what you need to say then you and the team might not get the best value out of the meeting. If you need to update the status on a task you are working on, do so before the Daily Scrum. It will help if Development Team members ensure that the Sprint Backlog or Sprint progress (burn-down charts) is up to date before the Daily Scrum.

Sprint Review

Overview

The Sprint Review is an event, an informal meeting held near the end of the Sprint before time-box expires, to inspect the Increment and adapt the Product Backlog if needed. Sprint results are discussed in the Sprint Review. Scrum Team and stakeholders inspect the outcome of a Sprint and figure out what to do next. All members of the Scrum Team should be present so that they can hear the feedback from all attendees and can answer questions regarding the Product Increment. Sprint Review focuses on the product itself, and Product Owner may decide to release the Product Increment as per business need. This is at most a four-hour meeting for one-month Sprints. For shorter Sprints, the event is usually shorter.

Sprint Review is not a status meeting. All members review the Product Increment, and their feedback is added into Product Backlog for future implementation in upcoming Sprints.

During the Sprint Review, the Scrum Team and stakeholders collaborate about what was done in the Sprint. Based on that and any changes to the Product Backlog during the Sprint, attendee collaborates on the next things that could be done to optimize value.

Presentation of the Increment is intended to elicit feedback and foster collaboration.

Scrum Team decides who leads the meeting and who demonstrates the work done. Usually, the Scrum Master facilitates this meeting. The Scrum Master ensures that the event takes place and that attendees understand its purpose. The Scrum Master teaches everyone involved to keep it within the time-box. The Product Owner starts the meeting by summarizing the Sprint results (what was the planned Sprint Goal, Product Backlog Items have been Done and what has not been Done). The Development Team demonstrates the work done, and every member should get a chance to the demonstration on a rotational basis. There are no rules as such!

The Sprint Review includes the following elements:

- Attendees include the Scrum Team and stakeholders. The Scrum Team decide who all should attend the Sprint Review meeting, and the Product Owner sends the invitation to stakeholders.

- The Product Owner explains what Product Backlog Items have been Done and what has not been Done.

- The Development Team discusses what went well during the Sprint, what problems it ran into, and how those problems were solved.

- The Development Team demonstrates the work that it has Done and answers questions about the Increment.

- The Product Owner discusses the Product Backlog as it stands. He or she projects likely target and delivery dates based on progress to date (if needed).

- The entire group collaborates on what to do next so that the Sprint Review provides valuable input to subsequent Sprint Planning.

- Review of how the marketplace or potential use of the product might have changed what is the most valuable thing to do next.

- Review of the timeline, budget, potential capabilities, and marketplace for the next anticipated releases of functionality or capability of the product.

The result of the Sprint Review is a revised Product Backlog that defines the probable Product Backlog Items for the next Sprint. The Product Backlog may also be adjusted overall to meet new opportunities.

The Sprint Review is a mandatory event, even if the Scrum Team does not have anything to show at the Sprint Review. The feedback from the stakeholders can determine how to best move forward for the next Sprint.

Participants

- Scrum Team – The Product Owner, Scrum Master, and Development Team.

- Stakeholders – The Stakeholders have a formal role in the process only during the Sprint Review. The product Owner invites stakeholders such as the sales team, marketing team, customers, end-users, and so on.

Inputs

Inputs to the Sprint Review are:

- Sprint Backlog

- Sprint Goal

- Product Increment

- Product Backlog

- Impediments that stakeholders can help resolve

Outputs

Outputs of the Sprint Review are:

- Updated Product Backlog

- Updated Release Plan

Recommendations

- Product Owner should start the Sprint Review and inform everyone about what is achieved as the Sprint results (Product Backlog Items that have been Done and what has not been Done).

- If the goal is not met, then everyone should focus on the best course of action for moving forward.

- It is a myth that Sprint Review is just a Demo or just a presentation of what is done and what is not done.

- In this meeting, the team should discuss and identify the problems. However, the resolution should be made in some other meetings.

- The Sprint Review should not be considered as a traditional milestone sign-off (from the business) meeting.

Sprint Retrospective

Overview

The Sprint Retrospective is a formal opportunity for the Scrum Team to inspect itself and create a plan for improvements to be enacted during the next Sprint. The Sprint is concluded with a Sprint Retrospective.

The Sprint Retrospective occurs after the Sprint Review and before the next Sprint Planning.

This is at most a three-hour meeting for one-month Sprints. For shorter Sprints, the event is usually shorter.

The meeting is basically about establishing what went well, where there is room for improvement, and what experiments might be usefully conducted to learn and build a better product.

The Scrum Master facilitates Sprint Retrospective and ensures that the event takes place and that attendants understand its purpose. The Scrum Master ensures that the meeting is positive and productive. The Scrum Master teaches all to keep it within the time-box. The Scrum Master participates as a peer team member in the meeting from the accountability over the Scrum process. Scrum Team should keep the Retrospective with fun. As Development Team matures, they must think of Retrospective formats themselves. They can support the Scrum Master with creative, fun, and useful formats and offer to facilitate the sessions themselves.

The purpose of the Sprint Retrospective is to:

- Inspect how the last Sprint went with regards to people, relationships, processes, and tools.

- Identify and order the major items that went well and potential improvements.

- Create a plan for implementing improvements to the way the Scrum Team does its work.

The Scrum Master encourages the Scrum Team to improve, within the Scrum process framework, its development process, and practices to make it more effective and enjoyable for the next Sprint.

During each Sprint Retrospective, the Scrum Team plans ways to increase product quality by improving work processes or adapting the definition of Done, if appropriate and not in conflict with product or organizational standards.

By the end of the Sprint Retrospective, the Scrum Team should have identified improvements that it will implement in the next Sprint. During Sprint Retrospective, the participants also discuss and examine the actions taken on improvements identified from the last Retrospective. Implementing these improvements in the next Sprint is the adaptation to the inspection of the Scrum Team itself. Although improvements may be implemented at any time, the Sprint Retrospective provides a formal opportunity to focus on inspection and adaptation.

In the next Sprint, to ensure continuous improvement, Sprint Backlog should include at least one high priority process improvement identified.

Participants

- All members of the Development Team

- The Scrum Master. The Scrum Master participates as a Scrum Team member

- The Product Owner. The Product Owner participates as a Scrum Team member.

- Non-Scrum Team Members - The Sprint Retrospective is a private event for the Scrum Team. External influences like stakeholders, managers, and others outside the Scrum Team must not attend the Sprint Retrospective. They should attend a Retrospective only if invited by the Scrum Team.

Inputs

Inputs to the Sprint Retrospective are:

- Processes used by the Scrum team during the current Sprint.

- Useful data collected during the Sprint, which participants will use for brainstorming.

- Improvement action items recorded from previous Retrospectives

- Definition of Done

Outputs

Outputs of the Sprint Retrospective are:

- Improvement action items for the upcoming Sprints.

- Impediments identified.

- List of ideas gathered during the current Retrospective that is not converted into improvement action items, but Scrum team might use this list of ideas in the future.

Recommendations

- Before closing the Retrospective, it is a good practice to ask participants for any suggestions to improve in performing a Retrospective next time.

- After closing the Sprint Retrospective, it is essential that participants work on the improvement actions in the upcoming Sprints.

Sample Questions

Q: The most important opportunity for capturing lessons learned is

1. Sprint Learning
2. Sprint Retrospective
3. Sprint Review
4. Daily Scrum

Q: An organization Kremlin Corp is developing a new product with two weeks of Sprint length. A Scrum Team (7 Development Team, Michelle Scrum Master, and Natasha Product Owner) is new to Scrum. After completing the first week, the Natasha tells Michelle that she feels Development Team is not able to complete the selected PBIs. What will Michelle do? Select all applicable.

1. Michelle tells Natasha that she should have patients and allow Development Team to do their job.
2. Development Team members are self-organized. Michelle inform Natasha that it is up to the Development Team to fulfill the commitment of selected PBIs.
3. Development Team is committed to Sprint Goal and not to the PBIs. Michelle Coaches Natasha, more work may appear during the Sprint execution as more clarity is learned. Hence, the prediction of selected PBIs cannot be considered as a commitment.
4. Michelle should add more developers to the Development Team.

Q: What all can be discussed in Sprint Planning? Select all applicable

1. Sprint Goal
2. Product Goal
3. Ordering the Product Backlog Items
4. How the chosen work can be done

Q: Who invites external stakeholders for the Sprint Review meeting?

1. Scrum Master
2. Development Team
3. Product Owner
4. Scrum Team

Q: What is the role of Scrum Master in Sprint Retrospective meeting?

1. Silent Observer
2. Peer Team member
3. Retrospective Reviewer
4. External Observer

Q: What is the last event in a Sprint?

1. Sprint Planning
2. Sprint Retrospective
3. Sprint Windup
4. Daily Scrum
5. Sprint Review

Q: Which of the following is not an input to the Sprint Planning Meeting? Select all applicable

1. Latest Product Increment
2. Sprint Backlog
3. The projected capacity of the Development Team
4. Past performance of the Development Team
5. Constraints & Impediments

Q: Items selected during the Sprint Planning meeting should not be re-negotiated during the Sprint. True or False

Q: Which of the following statements are true about Daily Scrum. Select all applicable

1. It is fifteen minutes or less in duration
2. All Scrum Team member must be present
3. Its location and time should remain constant
4. Its time should remain constant and location is not constant as per meeting room availability
5. All must stand up during Daily Scrum

Q: In which all Scrum events, a complete Scrum Team can participate. Select all applicable

1. Sprint Planning
2. Daily Scrum
3. Sprint Review
4. Sprint Execution
5. Sprint Retrospective

Q: Morgan, a fresh developer who is also new to Scrum asked Scrum Master Ralph which is the best place to have Daily Scrum meeting? Help yourself with your answer.

1. Wherever Ralph finds it suitable
2. Wherever the Development Team finds it suitable
3. Whichever room is available for meeting
4. All of the above

Q: Sprint Planning is a part of the Sprint. True or False

Q: Sprint Retrospective is a part of the Sprint. True or False

Q: A new developer, Gloria has joined four Sprints earlier. During the Daily Scrum, all developers were sharing with each other about their progress and if Sprint Goal is achievable or not. Only Gloria said she does not know when her task will get complete. What needs to be done in this scenario?

1. Scrum Master should teach Gloria on how to estimate the task
2. Scrum Master should inform Gloria's supervisor that she is not able to work on this project

3. Swap Gloria's task with some other developer to eliminate the risk of not meeting Sprint Goal

4. The Development Team should collaborate and pair Gloria with some other Developer to eliminate the risk of not meeting Sprint Goal

Q: A Scrum team of 7 developers, Scrum Master Thomas and Product Owner Rodney are developing one product with Sprint duration of two weeks. Six month is passed and Product Increments are delivered on time. However, in one of the Sprint, Rodney has found that the technical debt has increased and quality of the product started decreasing. To clear the debt, couple of more Sprints will be needed. What could be the possible reasons for increasing technical debt? Select all applicable.

1. As number of Sprints increases day by day it is obvious that technical debt will increase and hence after every six month one Sprint should be reserved for fixing the technical debt so that product quality can be increased.

2. The Development Team and Rodney are not having conversations around technical debt.

3. Thomas has not ensured that the Scrum Team is transparent.

4. All of the above

Q: There are some Scrum events where external people can attend the meetings. Help yourself in finding those Scrum events where external people to the Scrum Team can attend. Select all applicable

1. Sprint Planning
2. Sprint Celebration
3. Daily Scrum
4. Sprint Review
5. Sprint Retrospective

Q: Daniel is a Scrum Master for a distributed Development Team. Development Team has 7 developers, 3 working from India, 2 from US and 2 from the UK. It is obvious that with such a distributed team more coordination effort will be needed for arranging the Daily Scrum calls. To reduce the coordination efforts, the Development Team is planning to have Daily Scrum only on Wednesday because of distributed locations. What do you think Daniel should do?

1. Daniel should straight away disagree to Development Team's decision.

2. Scrum Teams are self-organized; Daniel should support Development Team's decision.

3. Daniel coach the Development Team to understand the purpose and benefits of Daily Scrum.

4. As an experiment, advice Development Team to change the Daily Scrum time-box to 10 minutes.

Q: In Sprint Planning meeting, the work to be performed in the Sprint is planned. This plan is created by the collaborative work of the entire Scrum Team. The team selects the Product Backlog Items it deems feasible for the Sprint considering the Definition of Done and the average work completed in previous Sprints. The User Stories at Sprint Planning should be well understood. What do you think Scrum Team should do to make User Stories more valuable during Sprint Planning?

1. Scrum Master will ensure that User stories are ready one Sprint ahead of time

2. The business analyst and senior developers of the Development Team should document high-ordered User Stories on daily basis

3. The Product Owner is responsible for Product Backlog hence he or she should prepare detailed User Stories and should not disturb the Development Team

4. The Development Team uses some time in each Sprint to analyze, and estimate high-ordered User Stories

Q: Product Backlog Items at Sprint Planning should be well understood. All the Product Backlog Items that are selected for a particular Sprint are necessarily supposed to be broken down into smaller Product Backlog Items that can be implemented in couple of hours, and at the end of the Sprint Planning the Development Team should know all details about them. True or False

Q: Help yourself in answering what is Sprint Review. Select all applicable

1. Opportunity for Development Team to connect with stakeholders
2. Formal sign-off of Product Increment from the Product Owner and Scrum Master
3. Scrum Master reviewing work done by the Product Owner
4. None of the above

Q: Sprint Review is an informal meeting to present the working shippable Product Increment and get the feedback. True or False

Q: Sprint Review is a formal meeting with the stakeholders to show the work done during the Sprint. True or False

Q: Sprint Review and Sprint Retrospective are the only two events held on the last day of the Sprint. True or False

Q: The Scrum Team should choose at least one low priority process improvement, identified during the Sprint Retrospective, and place it in the Product Backlog. True or False

Q: The best time in the day for conducting Daily Scrum meeting is morning. True or False

Q: In Sprint Planning meeting, the number of items selected from the Product Backlog for the Sprint is solely up to the Development Team. Could the Sprint Planning be completed if only work planned for the first days of the Sprint is broken down into units of one day or less. True or False

Q: Which of the following are discussed in the Sprint Review meeting. Select all applicable

1. The Product Owner explains what Product Backlog Items have been Done and what has not been Done
2. Review of the deliverable product
3. Product Owner reviews the available budget and timeline
4. Development team demonstrates the work done and what has not done in the Sprint
5. The Development Team discusses what went well during the Sprint, what problems it ran into, and how those problems were solved

Q: In Sprint Planning, who eventually decides when the Development Team has enough work for the Sprint?

1. The Scrum Master
2. On rotation basis it should be done by the developer
3. The Product Owner
4. The Development Team

Q: Which is the first event when a Sprint starts?

1. Daily Scrum
2. Sprint Planning
3. Sprint Startup
4. Sprint Review
5. Sprint Retrospective

Q: The Scrum Team should choose at least one high priority process improvement, identified during the Sprint Retrospective, and place it in the Sprint Backlog. True or False

Q: What is the main objective of Sprint Review? Select all applicable

1. To inspect the Product Increment and adapt the Product Backlog if needed
2. All change request should be reviewed in Sprint Review, as Product Backlog cannot be changed without a change request to the Product Owner
3. Presentation to senior management
4. Sprint Review is a status meeting in which all developers will get a chance to speak
5. As name suggest it is a review of entire Sprint

Q: How many sessions do you have in Sprint Planning meeting?

1. One
2. Three
3. Two
4. Four

Q: A junior developer Taylor who is new to Scrum asked one question to Scrum Master George. Taylor said, as per Scrum Guide the Daily Scrum should always take exactly 15 minutes. If we (Development Team) managed to do Daily Scrum in 10 minutes, should we spend 5 minutes more on some useful team activities like Product Backlog Refinement, etc. as time-box is not expired yet? George asked Taylor, what you think Development Team should do. Taylor said, we would continue until time-box of 15 minutes expires. Do you agree with Taylor? Yes or No.

Q: The Scrum Team should choose at least one high priority process improvement, identified during the Sprint Retrospective, and place it in the Product Backlog. True or False

Q: Candice a new developer has a question on Sprint Planning meeting. She asked Scrum Master Alexandra one scenario – Suppose in one Sprint Planning meeting, Scrum Team determined the top ordered

User Stories to be developed in the Sprint. We (The Development Team) pulled work into the Sprint Backlog from the Product Backlog. At the end of the meeting, we could break the User Stories for only the first few days of the Sprint. What should we do out of the following options. Help yourself in finding out what should Alexandra suggest. Select all applicable

1. The Development Team should continue Sprint Planning next day before they start the development
2. The Development Team should held daily Sprint Planning meeting to forecast what can be done on daily basis
3. The Development Team should close the Sprint Planning and start working on Sprint Backlog Items
4. Alexandra should coach the Development Team on how to decompose all items before time-box of Sprint Planning expires

Q: Which of the following statements are true about Sprint Retrospective? Select all applicable

1. Sprint Retrospective provides an informal opportunity to focus on inspection and adaptation.
2. In Sprint Retrospective, the team can discuss on the way the Scrum Team does Sprint Planning
3. Team can discuss on skills needed to improve the Development Team's ability to deliver
4. All of the above

Q: External influences like stakeholders, managers, and others outside the Scrum Team must attend the Sprint Retrospective. True or False

Q: As per Scrum Guide, Daily Scrum format is fixed - every developer must answer the three main questions: What was done yesterday? What will be done today? Are there any impediments? True or False

Q: It is not mandatory that all Development Team members are required to join the Sprint Planning meeting. True or False

Q: Help yourself in identifying the latest step in the sequence out of the following events.

1. Daily Scrum
2. Sprint Retrospective
3. Sprint Planning
4. Sprint Review

Q: The Scrum Team should choose at least one high priority process improvement, identified during the Sprint Retrospective, and place it in the Process Improvement Backlog. True or False

Q: As per Scrum, which one of the following is true about Daily Scrum meeting? Select all applicable

1. Performance of each developer is discussed and reviewed
2. The meeting must be kept short and well structured
3. Meeting should not be started unless all developers joins
4. Time-box for Daily Scrum is 15 minutes. Half duration of Daily Scrum should be utilized in morning and remaining half in evening

Q: Everyone must stand for Daily Scrum to keep the meeting short. True or False

Q: In Daily Scrum meeting, problems are discussed and resolved. No developer should leave the meeting until the problem is resolved even if problem is not related to that developer. True or False

Q: What is the primary objective of the Sprint Review? Select all applicable

1. The primary objective of the Sprint Review is to demo the Sprint work to each other so that everyone will be on the same page before Sprint Retrospective
2. The primary objective of the Sprint Review is to demo the Sprint work and to receive feedback from the Product Owner on the work completed

3. The primary objective of the Sprint Review is to demo the Sprint work and to receive feedback from the Scrum Master on the work completed

4. The primary objective of the Sprint Review is to demo the Sprint Backlog to all stakeholders

Q: Select the mandatory questions that are asked in the Daily Scrum meeting. Select all applicable.

1. What was done yesterday
2. What will be done today
3. Are there any impediments
4. None of the above
5. All of the above

Q: In a Scrum training, a developer Gigi asked a question – for which all groups the Sprint Review is an inspect and adapt opportunity?

1. Review Team
2. The Scrum Team and stakeholders
3. The Scrum Team
4. Stakeholders
5. Only Development Team

Q: The Sprint Goal and Sprint Backlog are the result of the Sprint Planning. True or False?

Q: Which topics should be discussed in the Sprint Review?

1. No discussions, demonstration of Done and not Done work
2. Sprint Results
3. No discussions, only demonstration of Done work
4. Performance of each developer

Q: In which meetings, the Key Stakeholders are allowed to participate?

1. The Sprint Review
2. The Sprint Planning

3. Stakeholder Review meeting
4. All of the above

Q: Select the two meetings in which people outside the Scrum Team are allowed to participate.

1. The Sprint Review
2. The Sprint Planning
3. Stakeholder review meeting
4. The Sprint Retrospective

Q: What is the result of the Sprint Review?

1. A revised Product Backlog with user Stories for the next Sprint
2. A list of improvements that the Scrum Team can implement in the next Sprint. At least one top priority improvement is added in Sprint Backlog
3. Both 1 & 2
4. None of the above

Q: Sprint Goal and Sprint Backlog are the output of Sprint Planning meeting. Sprint Backlog Items are freezes after the Sprint Planning. True or False

Q: Stakeholders are external to the Scrum Team. The Product Owner should interact with stakeholders regularly to keep them aware of the product's progress. Do you agree with this? Yes or No

Q: Select which all things happens from following in Daily Scrum. Select all applicable

1. Development team plans work for the next 12 hours
2. Inspect Development Team's work since last week's Daily Scrum
3. Tracking and Commitment of remaining Sprint work
4. None of the above

Q: A Development Team of 7 members is working on a project from last six months. Sprint duration is of two weeks. In a Sprint Review, the stakeholder Roger observes that product development progress is not clear and transparent. What do you think, who is responsible for this?

1. Development team
2. Scrum Team
3. Product Owner
4. Scrum Master

Q: Who all are allowed to participate in the Daily Scrum?

1. The Product Owner
2. The Development Team
3. The Key Stakeholders
4. The Scrum Master

Q: The Daily Scrum time-box depends on the size of the Development team. True or False

Q: How much is the time-box for Sprint Planning meeting?

1. Not more than 8 hours for two week Sprint
2. Not more than 4 hours
3. As much as Development Team need, as they are self-organized
4. 8 hours and longer as needed
5. None of the above

Q: Which Scrum event is an opportunity for inspection and adaption? Select all applicable

1. Daily Scrum
2. Sprint Retrospective
3. Sprint Review
4. Sprint Planning

Q: Burn-down chart shows how much work remains until the end of the Sprint. True or False

Q: The purpose of the Sprint Retrospective is to get feedback from the key stakeholders invited by the Product Owner. True or False

Q: What is the purpose of the Sprint Retrospective. Select all applicable

1. Inspect how the last Sprint went with regards to people, relationships, processes, and tools.
2. The Development Team demonstrates the work that it has Done and answers questions about the Increment.
3. Identify and order the major items that went well and potential improvements.
4. Create a plan for implementing improvements to the way the Scrum Team does its work.

Q: What is the input to the Sprint Planning?

1. Past performance of the Development Team
2. Feedback from the Organization CEO
3. The Product Backlog
4. The latest product Increment
5. Feedback from the Key Stakeholders
6. The projected capacity of the Development Team during the Sprint

Q: What are the questions the Sprint Planning answers? Select two.

1. What can be delivered in the Increment resulting from the upcoming Sprint?
2. Who is responsible for Sprint Backlog Items?
3. Who is responsible for release plan?
4. How will the work needed to deliver the Increment be achieved?

Q: Who participates in the Sprint Planning? Select all applicable

1. Sprint Planner
2. The Development Team
3. The Scrum Master
4. The Key Stakeholders
5. The Product Owner

Q: Who participates in the Sprint Review? Select all applicable

1. The Product Owner
2. The Scrum Master
3. The Testing Team
4. The Development Team
5. The Key Stakeholders

Q: Select the correct statement about Sprint Retrospective.

1. An event to inspect the Increment and adapt the Product Backlog if needed
2. An event for the Scrum Team to inspect itself and adapt the Product Backlog if needed
3. An event to review Sprint Backlog and add at least one top priority continuous improvement in Sprint Backlog
4. None of the above

Q: Sprint Planning can be attended by other individuals than the Scrum Team to provide technical or domain guidance. True or False

Q: Select from following that guides to the Development Team on why it is building the Product Increment.

1. The Scrum Master
2. The Product Owner
3. The Sprint Backlog
4. All of the above
5. None of the above

Q: The Sprint Goal guides to the Product Owner on why it is building the Product Increment.

Q: Kento, a new developer was discussing with his friends from other Scrum team that his Scrum Master Tom is not attending Sprint Planning meetings. One of his friend Robert said that only the Product Owner and the Development Team participate in the Sprint Planning. There is nothing to do for the Scrum Master. Do you agree with Robert? Yes or No

Q: At the Sprint Retrospective meeting, the Scrum Team identified some improvements that can be done. Select the true statement from following. Select the best option.

1. Plan one Sprint for improvements before technical debt starts increasing.
2. Make sure the Sprint Backlog for the next Sprint includes at least one low priority process improvement.
3. Make sure the Product Backlog for the next Sprint includes all the top priority improvements.
4. Observe the improvement area for couple of Sprints and then decide if any action needed on improvement identified.
5. None of the above.

Q: Who is responsible for creating the Sprint Goal at Sprint Planning?

1. The Development Team
2. The Scrum Team
3. The Product Owner
4. The Scrum Master

Q: What is the maximum length of the Sprint Review?

1. 15 minutes per day
2. 4 hours and longer as needed

3. 4 hours for a monthly Sprint. For shorter Sprints, it is usually shorter

4. As long as needed for self-organizing Development Team

Q: The time-box for a Daily Scrum is.

1. The same time of day every day

2. 15 minutes for a 4-week Sprint. For shorter Sprints, it is usually shorter

3. 2 minutes per team member.

4. As per team size.

5. None of the above

Q: What pre-conditions must be met to enable Sprint Planning to start?

1. Sign off from Product Owner for earlier Sprint

2. A Sprint Goal is defined and visible to all

3. Sufficient Product Backlog Items in "Ready" state

4. There are no such pre-conditions

Q: In Sprint Retrospective, Development Team provides feedback about Scrum Master and Product Owner for that Sprint to the management so that everyone can improve and collaborate to achieve the desired results. True or False

Q: Haruma, a junior developer new to Scrum wanted to know more about Daily Scrum. Help yourself in selecting the true statements about Daily Scrum.

1. The Product Owner identifies new impediments

2. The Scrum Master get the status from all developers

3. The Development Team holds this meeting to manage and follow up on its development work

4. Daily Scrum refines the Product Backlog

5. The Daily Scrum is an internal meeting for the Development Team

Q: What is the role of Scrum Master in Sprint Retrospective?

1. Silent Observer
2. Peer Team Member
3. Retrospective Reviewer
4. None of the above

Q: Which of the following might be discussed in Sprint Retrospective? Select all applicable

1. Processes used by the Scrum team during the current Sprint
2. Refining the Product Backlog
3. Define Sprint Goal for next Sprint
4. The Definition of Done

Q: During the Sprint Review, the Scrum Team and stakeholders collaborate about what was done in the Sprint and the project will be evaluated against which of the following.

1. Test Cases
2. Test Results
3. Sprint Goal
4. Sprint Planning

Q: A Development Team (of 9 developers) was not able to finish Daily Scrum in 15 minutes, hence they decided to split teams in two teams (for next 5 Sprints till they become proficient in completing the Daily Scrum in 15 minutes) as it was not possible for 9 developers to share their updates in 15 minutes. Do you agree with Development Team's decision? Yes or No

Chapter 9

Scrum Artifacts

Overview

Scrum's artifacts represent work or value that provides transparency and opportunities for inspection and adaptation. Artifacts defined by Scrum are specifically designed to maximize transparency of all information so that everybody has a similar understanding of the artifact.

Scrum Artifacts are:

- Product Backlog

- Sprint Backlog

- Increment

Scrum Teams must frequently inspect Scrum artifacts and progress to detect undesirable variances.

Product Backlog

The Product Backlog is an ordered list of everything that is known to be needed in the product. It is the single source of requirements for the product. The Product Backlog is composed of Product Backlog Items. PBIs can be in the form of functional or nonfunctional requirements, all new features, changes to the existing features, functionalities, requirements, ideas, enhancements, use cases, defects, maintenance work, architectural work, performance-related work, technical debt, security-related work, and so on that constitute the changes to be made to the product in future releases.

Defects can be directly added as a Product Backlog Item in Product Backlog or defect can be added in any defect tracking system while the reference of that defect can be added in Product Backlog.

Table 8: Example Product Backlog

Order	PBI Desc.	Area Name	State	Effort	Tag	Value
1	PBI 1	Area 1	Ready	8		500
2	PBI 2	Area 2	Ready	6		400
3	PBI 3	Area 1	Ready	7	Defect	300
4	PBI 4	Area 2	New	8		400
5	PBI 5	Area 3	New	4		500

Sample Product Backlog Items are:

- As a library user, I want to find book by title so that I can find all books with my searched titles

- Allow user to access and view reports for last one year.

- Improve page-loading time for login screen.

At the time of the creation of a Product Backlog Item on the Product Backlog, the item is clearly valuable for a customer. It provides a shared understanding of what to build and the order in which to build it. It is a highly visible artifact that is accessible to all project participants.

A Product Backlog is never complete. The earliest development of it lays out the initially known and best-understood requirements. Every item on the Product Backlog holds just enough detail to make it clear what the value represents. An item is intentionally incomplete to encourage additional and explicit discussion over it. Each item is a placeholder for discussion at the appropriate time. Continuously adhering to just enough descriptions and designs of the work, leaving out unnecessary details ensures that no excessive money and time is wasted if the item is ultimately being not created.

The Product Backlog evolves as the product and the environment in which it is used evolves. The Product Backlog is dynamic; it constantly changes to identify what the product needs to be appropriate, competitive, and useful. If a product exists, its Product Backlog also exists.

The Product Owner is responsible for the Product Backlog, including its content, availability, and ordering. Product Owner keeps the Product Backlog transparent for all the stakeholders.

Product Backlog Items have the attributes of

- Description
- Order
- Estimate
- Value

Product Backlog Items often include test descriptions that can prove its completeness when Done.

As a product is used and gains value, and the marketplace provides feedback, the Product Backlog becomes a larger and more exhaustive list.

Requirements never stop changing, so a Product Backlog is a living artifact. Changes in business requirements, market conditions, or technology may cause changes in the Product Backlog.

One product has one Product Backlog and one Product Owner. Multiple Scrum Teams often work together on the same product. One Product Backlog is used to describe the upcoming work on the product. A Product Backlog attribute that groups items may then be employed.

The most important items are always on top of the Product Backlog. Ordering is usually based on value, effort, dependencies, and risk. The Product Owner is accountable for ordering the Product

Backlog. Product Owner usually order the PBIs that can be taken for the upcoming Sprints. Time spent on detailing, estimating, and ordering PBIs that are never implemented is a waste of time.

Higher order Product Backlog Items are usually clearer and more detailed than lower ordered ones. Reasonably accurate estimates without being too precise are made based on the greater clarity and increased detail; the lower the order, the less detail, so some teams do not estimate them at all, or use T-shirt-size estimates like L, XL, XXL, etc. We need to find the proper balance of just enough and just in time breaking of larger PBIs into smaller PBIs. If we spend time on breaking items that are never going to be implemented, it is a waste of time. Contrary, if we do not break items, and Development Team wants to pull those items, Development Team spends their Sprint time in breaking those items or Product Owner may have to change the ordering of PBIs.

Product Backlog Items that will occupy the Development Team for the upcoming Sprint are refined so that any one item can reasonably be Done within the Sprint time-box. Product Backlog Items that can be Done by the Development Team within one Sprint are deemed "Ready" for selection in a Sprint Planning. Product Backlog Items usually acquire this degree of transparency through the above-described refining activities. The Product Backlog Item implementation is considered complete when there is no further work remaining to be done, as per the definition of Done, on the item to be released.

The Development Team is responsible for all estimates. The Product Owner may influence the Development Team by helping it understand and select trade-offs, but the people who perform the work make the final estimate.

At the Sprint Review, attendees collaborate on the next things that could be done to optimize the value, which is processed into an updated Product Backlog.

Monitoring Progress Toward Goals:

At any point in time, the total work remaining to reach a goal can be summed. The Product Owner tracks this total work remaining at least every Sprint Review. The Product Owner compares this amount with work remaining at previous Sprint Reviews to assess progress toward completing projected work by the desired time for the goal. This information is made available with transparency to all stakeholders in addition to the Scrum Team.

Various projective practices upon trending have been used to forecast progress, like burn-downs, burn-ups, or cumulative flows. These have proven useful. However, these do not replace the importance of empiricism. In complex environments, what will happen is unknown. Only what has already happened may be used for forward-looking decision-making.

Characteristics

Good Product Backlogs displays following characteristics:

- **D**etailed appropriately

- **E**mergent

- **E**stimated

- **P**rioritized

Roman Pichler (Pichler 2010) and Mike Cohn created the acronym DEEP. The DEEP criteria are useful for determining if a Product Backlog has been structured in the right way.

- Detailed Appropriately – Higher ordered Product Backlog Items are more detailed than lower ordered ones.

- Emergent – As long as a product exists, its Product Backlog also exists. The Product Backlog is, therefore, continually evolving.

When new items are added, or existing items are groomed, the Product Owner must reprioritize the Product Backlog Items

- Estimated – Higher orderd Product Backlog Items are more detailed and hence can be estimated. Product Backlog Items are estimated mostly either in story points or ideal days. Lower ordered items may or may not be estimated.

- Prioritized – The Product Owner order the Product Backlog Items usually based on the value

Product Backlog Refinement

Product Backlog Refinement, also called as grooming is the act of

- Adding details (creating and refining) to Product Backlog Items

- Estimating Product Backlog Items

- Ordering Product Backlog Items

The Product Owner and the Development Team do the refinement of the Product Backlog Items a couple of Sprints before the Sprint in which they are selected for implementation. The requirements are broken down to the level that is understandable by the Development Team in the Sprint Planning meeting. The level of granularity is dependent on the Development Team's understanding; hence, some requirements may not be broken down. Fine-grained requirements are only defined when they needed.

This is an ongoing process in which the Product Owner and the Development Team collaborate on the details of Product Backlog Items. Not only will new items regularly be added to your Product Backlog throughout the process, but also the priority of those items changes and shifts as you better understand your audience and product. During Product Backlog Refinement, items are reviewed and revised.

The Scrum Team decides how and when refinement is done. Experience shows that refinement usually consumes no more than 10% (10% is neither mandatory nor prescribed by Scrum Guide in any way) of the capacity of the Development Team. However, Product Backlog Items can be updated at any time by the Product Owner or at the Product Owner's discretion.

The Development Team may discuss architecture and infrastructure requirements during Product Backlog refinement and can add them to the Product Backlog.

The Product Owner is responsible for making sure that the grooming activities take place. Participants are:

- Product Owner
- Development Team
- Scrum Master
- Stakeholders (internal and external) – optional

Refinement may also happen in the same Sprint if they were not able to do it in the previous Sprints.

Definition of Ready

The Definition of Ready is a checklist of the work that must be completed before a Product Backlog Item can be declared in the ready state.

The Product Backlog Items at the top should be in the ready state to move to the Sprint Backlog.

Some teams can use the Definition of Ready and the Definition of Done as two states of Product Backlog Items.

An example of the Definition of Ready checklist is given below.

Table 9: Example Definition of Ready Checklist

SN	Checklist Items
1	PBI is small to complete in one or two days
2	Development Team is clear on the PBI, no pending queries are remaining
3	Acceptance criteria is available
4	Acceptance tests are defined

A strong Definition of Ready improves the Scrum team's chance of successfully meeting the Sprint Goal.

Estimation and Velocity

Estimation is how long it takes to develop what we are building. Estimates are not commitments, and it is important that we do not treat them as such committed deadlines. Velocity is the rate at which we get the work done. Velocity is not a measure of the value a team produces. Velocity tells you only how many units of work were completed and did not tell whether that work was valuable. Implementing a PBI of size 15 does not mean it will deliver more value than completing a PBI of size 10. We can forecast the product development duration by dividing the estimated size of a set of features by the team's velocity.

We should look at the business value that the team is delivering, instead of focusing on productivity. We should focus on removing impediments to improve the team's ability to deliver business value.

The most common units are story points and ideal days. Scrum Guide does not recommend any particular unit for PBI size estimation, and it is the team who decides which unit should be used.

The sum of the sizes of all the completed Product Backlog Items in a Sprint is the team's velocity for that Sprint. Velocity is calculated at the end of each Sprint. If a Product Backlog Item is not done or partially done, then, it is not included in the velocity. The velocity should always show the actual sum of sizes completed during the Sprint and should not be adjusted to show something that might have been achieved in ideal scenarios.

The number of Sprints needed in a release is determined by dividing the size of the release by the team's average velocity.

It is a good practice to express velocity as a range, for example, the velocity of 30 to 35 points each Sprint.

The new team forecasts the velocity for the Sprint as Development Team members have not worked together and have no historical data.

An example of relationship among size, velocity, and duration is given below.

- The sum of the PBI estimates for release 1 is 400 points. The team's average velocity for the prior eight Sprints is 30.

- To calculate the duration, we divide the size by the velocity. If the size of Release 1 is 400 points and the team can, on average, complete 30 points of work each Sprint, it should take the team 10 (400/30) Sprints to complete Release 1.

- Using a velocity range to do these calculations is more accurate than using an average velocity. If teams low velocity is 26 and high velocity is 30, release 1 needs 14 (400/30) to 16 Sprints (400/26).

Technical Debt

Technical debt is defined, as "anything that impedes agility as a product matures." Technical debt is not the same as the unfinished work. Technical debt refers to the shortcuts we purposely take to expedite the current situation, but it costs more soon. Technical debt certainly could be code-based, but it could also mean a lack of test automation and DevOps issues.

Technical debt affects transparency; as development progress and code is added, the system becomes more difficult to stabilize, which results in future work being slowed down in unpredictable ways. Technical debt leads to false assumptions about the current state of the Product Increment and may not be releasable at the end of a Sprint. Forecasting PBIs also become more difficult. Product cost starts increasing as technical debt increases, even for small changes need to pay more cost, which would have done at less price.

Technical debt could be because of architecture created only to resolve any particular issue at that moment or because of known bugs that could not be fixed due to time constraints, or because of incomplete testing.

If the technical debt keeps on continuously increasing, then the product may not meet the expectations. Some of the reasons for increasing technical debt are:

- The Development Team has not been paying enough attention to quality and is using shortcuts.

- The Development Team and the Product Owner are not discussing on technical debt.

- The Scrum Team is not using inspect and adapt events effectively.

- Scrum Team is not transparent, during their discussions, decisions, and demonstrations; and not imbibes one of the values – 'Openness' – of Scrum.

Technical Debt needs to be repaid should be added to the Product Backlog. Scrum does not prescribe any separate Sprint to remove the Technical Debt. If something that needs to be re-worked later, then it is seen as a waste. Scrum suggests altering the Definition of Done to include the non-creation of technical debt at the point of work done. Technical debt removal over time is important to the long-term viability of a product.

User Stories

A User Story is a very high-level definition of a requirement. It captures a description of a product feature from an end-user perspective. It shows the business value of the product features. The user story describes the type of user, what they want, and why. A user story should be short, usually fitting on a sticky note. They are simple and considered as a placeholder for conversations among stakeholders, Product Owner, and Development Team. User stories should be written in such a manner that both business people and technical people understand it easily.

User Story format:

As a <user role> I want to <goal> so that <benefit>

Example:

As a user I want to create a summary report of my data so that I can publish it to senior management.

User stories can give reference to some other documents, as the content of the referred document is not needed in the user story.

Example:

'As an HR I want to see employee report in graphical format. For more details, refer graphical report template V3.0 released by corporate on the configuration management server'.

A user story also contains the Acceptance Criteria.

Example:

As a library user I want to upload an eBook file to the eLibrary so that I can share it with all other users.

Condition of satisfaction:

Verify with .pdf file

Verify file size<=400 MB

Stories can exist at multiple levels of abstraction:

- Some teams call larger user stories as epics. They are usually months in size. Epics give a high-level overview of what is required. Epic is not very detailed as it is usually months in size. Epic can also be considered as a large collection of more detailed stories to be created in the future.

- Some teams call user stories that are too big for a single Sprint (usually weeks in size) as features. Some teams call a collection of related user stories as a theme.

- Stories are usually small in size that can be done in a Sprint.

Estimation Units

A Story Point is a common unit of measure for estimating the effort required to implement a user story (Product Backlog Item). It is a number that represents the difficulty level of the user story.

PBIs can also be estimated in ideal days.

INVEST

Bill Wake created the INVEST mnemonic for Agile software projects as a reminder of the characteristics of a good quality Product Backlog Item (commonly written in user story format, but not required to be).

The INVEST criteria are:

- **I**ndependent
- **N**egotiable

- **V**aluable

- **E**stimatable

- **S**mall

- **T**estable

Apply these attributes to create good stories.

- Independent – The PBI should be self-contained, in a way that there is no inherent dependency on another PBI. Stories are most comfortable to work with if they are independent. We should be able to move PBIs around without much effort. This is easily possible if they are independent. When applying the independent criteria, the goal is not to eliminate all dependencies, but instead to write stories in a way that minimizes dependencies.

- Negotiable – A good story is negotiable. A good story captures the essence, not the details. PBIs are not explicit contracts and should leave space for discussion. The PBI can be rewritten or even discarded, depending on the business, market, technical, or any other type of requirement by team members.

- Valuable – A PBI must deliver value to the Product Owner.

- Estimatable – Development Team must always be able to estimate the size of a PBI. If a PBI size cannot be estimated, it can never be planned or tasked; thus, it can never become part of an iteration. Therefore, there is no point in keeping this kind of PBI in the Product Backlog at all.

- Small – Stories worked on in Sprints should be small. Try to keep your PBI sizes to typically a few person-days and at most a few person-weeks. A good rule of thumb (neither mandatory nor prescribed by Scrum Guide in any way) is that any single Product Backlog Item that is to be implemented in upcoming

Sprints does not take more than 50% of an iteration. For example, a single item won't take more than 5 days for a 10-day Sprint.

- Testable – A good story is testable. Being testable means having proper acceptance criteria. If one cannot test a PBI due to a lack of information, the PBI should not be considered a good candidate to be part of the Sprint Backlog. Epic-size stories probably do not have tests associated with them. Stories for non-functional requirements (Ex. 100% uptime) may not have testable criteria.

Non Functional Requirements

Non-functional requirements describe the experience of the user while doing the work such as speed, security, uptime, response time, or accuracy. They are usually global constraints on the product that results in development cost and operational costs.

They can be written in a user story format or any other format.

User Story format:

As a user I want to receive a response to any input in less than one second so that many user will be active on the website.

Other format:

Response time must be less than one second for any input on the webpage.

Non-functional requirements are essential because they may affect the overall architecture of a product rather than the individual modules. For example, to ensure that performance requirements are met, you may have to develop the system to minimize communication between modules.

Usually, the nonfunctional requirement should be included in the Definition of Done.

Sprint Backlog

Overview

The Sprint Backlog is the set of Product Backlog Items selected for the Sprint, plus a plan (often a list of tasks) for delivering the product Increment and realizing the Sprint Goal.

The Sprint Backlog is created in Sprint Planning. It is a forecast by the Development Team about what functionality can be in the next Increment and the work needed to deliver that functionality into a Done Increment. Sprint Backlog can consist of tests, tasks, user cases, user stories, nonfunctional requirements, and so on.

The Sprint Backlog makes visible all the work that the Development Team identifies as necessary to meet the Sprint Goal. To ensure continuous improvement, it includes at least one high priority process improvement identified in the previous Retrospective meeting.

The Sprint Backlog is a plan with enough detail that changes in progress can be understood in the Daily Scrum.

The Development Team modifies the Sprint Backlog throughout the Sprint, and the Sprint Backlog emerges during the Sprint. This emergence occurs as the Development Team works through the plan and learns more about the work needed to achieve the Sprint Goal.

As new work is required, the Development Team adds it to the Sprint Backlog as soon as they are identified. As work is performed or completed, the estimated remaining work is updated. When elements of work identified during Sprint Planning meetings are deemed unnecessary, they are removed.

Only the Development Team can change its Sprint Backlog during a Sprint. The Sprint Backlog is a highly visible, real-time picture of the work that the Development Team plans to accomplish during the Sprint, and it belongs solely to the Development Team.

The Product Backlog can be shared among different teams if they are working on the same product; however, Sprint Backlog is specific and owned by a Development Team hence Sprint Backlog cannot be shared among different teams.

Monitoring Sprint Progress

- At any point in time in a Sprint, the total work remaining in the Sprint Backlog can be summed.

- The Development Team tracks this total work remaining at least for every Daily Scrum to project the likelihood of achieving the Sprint Goal.

- By tracking the remaining work throughout the Sprint, the Development Team can manage its progress.

Increment

The Increment also called Product Increment is the sum of all the Product Backlog Items completed during a Sprint and the value of the increments of all previous Sprints.

Each Increment is additive to all prior Increments and thoroughly tested, ensuring that all increments work together.

The Increment, the sum of all previous Increments as all the previous work, is required for the Increment done to have value and to be potentially releasable. An Increment must be tested adequately.

The Increment must be integrated into the existing Product Increment during the Sprint, and collectively, it must be potentially releasable.

At the end of a Sprint, the new Increment must be Done, which means it must be in useable condition and meet the Scrum Team's definition of Done.

An Increment is a body of inspectable, done work that supports empiricism at the end of the Sprint.

The Increment must be in useable condition regardless of whether the Product Owner decides to release it. The Product Owner decides on releasing the Product Increment to production when it makes sense.

The Increment is a step toward a vision or goal.

Sample Questions

Q: When are the changes are allowed in the Product Backlog? Select the true statements from following. Select all applicable

1. The Product Backlog can be updated anytime by the Stakeholders
2. Changes in business requirements, market conditions, or technology does not cause changes to the Product Backlog
3. The Product Backlog is frozen when a Sprint is in progress
4. The Product Backlog can be updated anytime by the Sprint Owner
5. None of the above

Q: The product is always released after every Sprint. True or False

Q: Sprint Goal is fixed across Sprints and does not change. True or False

Q: What is constant across the Sprints? Select all applicable

1. Development team composition
2. Product Backlog
3. Sprint Goal
4. Velocity
5. None of the above

Q: The Development Team commits to the Sprint Goal. True or False

Q: In a startup organization, Visvarupa SoftTech a new Scrum Team is formed to work on a new product development. Five Sprints of two weeks each are completed successfully. The current velocity of a Scrum team is 20 units, which is as per expectations. As per the market's demand for the product, it is decided to add one more team to work on the same product. Which of the following statements are true. Select all applicable.

1. There might not be any impact on velocity, and it is 20
2. Velocity might increase

3. Product quality increases

4. If a Product Backlog Item is not Done or partially Done then it is not included in the velocity

5. Velocity might decrease

Q: Product Backlog is visible to the Scrum team as well as to the entire organization. True or False

Q: Sprint Backlog is visible to the Scrum team as well as to the entire organization. True or False

Q: Scrum suggests, there should be a separate Backlog Refinement session apart from Scrum events. True or False

Q: When can the Development Team add tasks for the user stories during the Sprint?

1. Sprint Planning is the event for identifying the tasks. Hence, it should be done only in this event.

2. Product Owner and Scrum Master are responsible for project outcome. Hence, whenever they ask Development Team to do so.

3. During Backlog Grooming.

4. As soon as possible, after they are identified, unless they change the scope of the Sprint Goal.

Q: User Story is one of the Scrum artifacts. True or False

Q: Gerard is a new comer in Development Team, he wanted to know about which all of the following operations on the Product Backlog Items Product Owner is responsible. Select all applicable

1. Content

2. Availability

3. Assignment

4. None of the above

Q: Velocity consist of units of work done as well as units of incomplete work at the end of the Sprint. True or False

Q: All Scrum teams in an organization should standardize their estimation techniques so that senior management can use team velocities to compare productivity of one Scrum team with other (comparison between projects with similar complexity and Scrum team size). True or False

Q: Technical debt leads to false assumptions about the current state of the system, specifically of an Increment being releasable at the end of a Sprint. True or False

Q: Select true statements from the following about the technical debt. Select all applicable

1. Technical debt leads to false assumptions about the current state of the Product Increment and may not be releasable at the end of a Sprint.
2. Product cost starts increasing as technical debt decreases
3. As development progresses and code is added, the system becomes more difficult to stabilize, which results in future work being slowed down in unpredictable ways.
4. Technical debt affects the technical expertise in team

Q: In Scrum, Team Velocity is a useful metric to track the progress of product development. Yes or No

Q: User Stories are represented as Product Backlog Items in Product Backlog. Defects are also represented in the Product Backlog. True or False

Q: While working on a new product development, the Development Team completed 8 User Stories and could partially complete two User Stories in a Sprint. Scrum team decided to put those two User Stories in the next Sprint. The story points for these two stories must be reduced (as some work was already completed in the earlier Sprint) to represent the remaining effort required to complete them. True or False

Q: Which of the following statements about Daily Scrum is true? Select all applicable

1. The Development Team updates the actual vs. planned progress report in the Daily Scrum meeting, which is used to update the status report.
2. Daily Scrum is the first meeting of the day the Development Team starts with.
3. Daily Scrum can be done multiple time in a day as per project need.
4. None of the above.

Q: Sprint Goal is measurable. True or False

Q: Product Owner is responsible for updating Product Backlog and it is an ever-evolving artifact, Development Team creates the Sprint Backlog at the start of the Sprint, and remains unchanged throughout the ongoing Sprint. True or False

Q: Sprint Planning is the act of adding details, estimates, and order to the Product Backlog Items in the Product Backlog.

Q: A Product Backlog can be considered complete if all the Product Backlog Items are ordered, estimated, and all the details about them are provided. True or False

Q: Scrum Team should start the new Sprint only if enough number of Product Backlog Items are well enough understood to make a complete forecast for the Sprint, else they should wait till sufficient Product Backlog Items are made available. True or False

Q: Like a Sprint Backlog, Product Backlog can also be shared among different teams if they are working on the same product – True or False

Q: User Story Point system is the best technique and is recommended way for estimating User Stories for all the Scrum teams – True or False

Q: When does the Product Backlog cease to exist?

1. When the Product Owner wishes
2. When the Development Team wishes
3. When the complete product is developed and released
4. When the product ceases to exist

Q: Velocity of multiple teams working on the same product cannot be compared. True or False

Q: One most important characteristic of a Product Backlog Item that is necessary to consider it for selection in Sprint is:

1. It should be marked as Ready
2. It should be ordered
3. It can be completed in one Sprint
4. It should be approved by Product Owner

Q: If there are unplanned leaves by two members of a 6-member Development Team for half of the Sprint, the actual velocity achieved at the end of the Sprint should be adjusted accordingly – True or False

Q: Does the Product Backlog contain only functional requirements for the Product? Yes or No

Q: When does the velocity for a Sprint calculated?

1. When the Sprint is over
2. At the end of every working day
3. Anytime during a Sprint
4. In Daily Scrum

Q: A Product Backlog Item (low order or high order), should possess sufficient detail for the Development Team to complete in a Sprint. True or False

Q: Which of the following statements best describes User Stories? Select all applicable

1. Poorly defined User Stories should be put with a lower order on the Product Backlog
2. Poorly defined User Stories should be kept out from the Product Backlog until sufficient detail is known
3. User Stories should be maintained in word file
4. User Stories should be maintained in excel file

Q: Accumulating technical debt does not impact the customer's value delivery. True or False

Q: What are the two primary artifacts of a Sprint Planning meeting?

1. A Sprint Goal and a Sprint Backlog
2. A Sprint Goal and a Product Backlog
3. Product Backlog and Sprint Plan
4. Sprint Backlog and Product Backlog

Q: Sprint Goal is only a forecast and not a commitment, it may change within the Sprint as more details are learned. True or False

Q: Select one best description from following for the User Stories

1. User Story even lower order should be defined well enough to be completed during a Sprint.
2. All User Stories are defined in Sprint Planning meeting of earlier Sprint.
3. Lower order User Stories can be refined as their priority increases.
4. Lower order User Stories are assigned to junior developers so that even if they are not completed will not affect Product Increment.

Q: What does Development Team do in Sprint Planning meeting from the following?

1. The Development Team should break each User Story into tasks and estimate the efforts for each task.

2. The Scrum Master assigns each User Story to the developer who is expert in that User Story.

3. The Development Team plan the sequence of Scrum events for the current Sprint.

4. All of the above.

Q: Bugs are tracked separately and are not part of the Product Backlog. True or False

Q: In Chitta Corp a new Scrum Team started developing a product. Four Sprints completed successfully and team has adopted Scrum practices and started enjoying the work in Agile way of working. A stakeholder Sarah was using the developed Product Increment while working on it, she got some idea on a new feature, and hence she decided to modify the Product Backlog. What is the best option for Sarah?

1. Sarah can request Scrum Master to modify Product Backlog

2. Sarah can modify the Product Backlog directly

3. Sarah can ask Development Team to update the Product Backlog

4. None of the above

Q: Who assigns User Stories to the Development Team members?

1. Scrum Master

2. On rotation basis done by each developer

3. Poker is used in Scrum for user story assignment

4. There is no assignment, and team pulls up the stories

Q: The existence of technical debt indicates insufficient development techniques and methods. True or False

Q: Who is the owner of the Product Backlog?

1. Product Backlog Owner

2. Development Team

3. Scrum Team

4. None of the above

Q: Who decides how and when to do the Product Backlog Refinement?

1. Product Owner

2. Development Team

3. Scrum Team

4. Recommended approach is to do it after Daily Scrum

5. It can happen daily and anyone can decide

Q: What does a Burndown chart shows?

1. The remaining days (estimated days) to complete before the Sprint end

2. The amount of work remaining (estimated efforts) during a Sprint

3. The amount of work (story points or ideal days) completed in a Sprint

4. The amount of hours has been spent during the Sprint.

5. None of the above

Q: When should separate Product Backlogs are maintained?

1. One Product Owner has one Product Backlog. Hence if there are several Product Owners for one product, each Product Owner should have their Product Backlog

2. Approved User Stories are maintained in Primary Product Backlog, newly identified User Stories should be kept in Backup Product Backlog before they get approved at all levels

3. If multiple teams are working on the independent features of the same product, each team can have an separate Product Backlog

4. None of the above

Q: What is an Increment?

1. The sum of Product Backlog Items in the Product Backlog that are Done and can be released
2. The sum of all the Sprint Backlog Items completed during the Sprint and the value of the Increments of all previous Sprints
3. Features completed and are in a usable state added to those delivered in the previous Sprints
4. All of the above
5. Both 2 & 3

Q: Where are the customer requirements stored?

1. In the Product Backlog
2. In the Sprint Backlog
3. In a database
4. In a Scrum Product Requirement Specification

Q: During Product Backlog Refinement, the following is added to the Product Backlog Items. Select all applicable

1. Detail
2. Value
3. Estimates
4. Order

Q: Can Scum Master create a Product Backlog Item? Yes or No

Q: Which of the following is not a Scrum artifact?

1. Sprint Goal
2. Sprint Backlog
3. Product Backlog
4. Increment

Q: Development Team has developed and delivered successful Product Increment on time. Can Product Owner choose not to release the product even if there are no bugs in the product. Yes or No

Q: Who defines the Sprint Backlog scope?

1. Product Owner
2. Development Team
3. Scrum Master
4. Key Stakeholders
5. All of the above

Q: According to Scrum, in what unit of time team plan Sprint activities?

1. Weeks
2. Days
3. Hours
4. Minutes

Q: When many Development Teams are working on the same product, is all of their Increments be integrated every Sprint?

1. Yes
2. No
3. Yes, but only the Development Teams whose work has dependencies
4. No, for less than one week Sprint

Q: Product Backlog should be reprioritized under which of the following situations? Select all applicable

1. The Product Owner should reprioritize the Product Backlog only at the starts of a new Sprint
2. The Scrum Team should reprioritize the Product Backlog whenever new information is learned
3. The Product Owner should reprioritize the Product Backlog whenever new information is learned
4. When new Sprint Goal is defined, Development should reprioritize the Product Backlog

Q: In Dhriti Soft organization, a Development Team of 6 members has completed six Sprints. In Sprint 1: 10 story points, Sprint 2: 11 story points, Sprint 3: 15 story points, Sprint 4: 14 story points, Sprint 5: 15 story points, Sprint 6: 10 story points are completed. 42 story points are remaining. What is the approximate number of Sprint required to complete product development?

1. 6
2. 5
3. 4
4. 3

Q: In a multi-national organization, a Development Team after completing a project (which was executed using Agile), has joined a new Scrum project. Scrum Team has started defining Product Backlog Items. The Scrum Master Bernard, observes that the team is not using the User Story format to capture the Product Backlog Items. What should Bernard do?

1. Teach the Development Team on how to write User Stories
2. Correct the Development Team's behavior by coaching them about User Stories
3. Bernard should allow the team to decide the format of the Product Backlog Items
4. Bernard should approach other Scrum teams in the organization and take help from other specialist for writing the user stories, once the Development Team learns how to write user stories, team can start writing of their own

Q: A new developer Francoise, says that all work to be done by the Development Team must eventually come from the Product Backlog. Do you agree with her? Yes or No

Q: A Product Owner can measure team's success by an increase in the team's velocity (number of developers are same as in earlier Sprints). True or False

Q: In the first Sprint, Scrum Team has completed 30 user story points at the end of week 1 of a two-week Sprint. What should be the velocity of the team?

1. 30
2. 15
3. 60
4. Can't say

Q: Velocity is a useful measure to compare two or more Scrum team's performance. True or False

Q: Velocity is a useful measure of the value a Scrum team produces. True or False

Q: When more than one Scrum Team is working on a single project. A separate Product Backlog is created for each Scrum Team and all of the Increments are integrated at the end in an integration Sprint. True or False

Q: Who is ultimately responsible for the Product Backlog Item estimates?

1. The Development Team
2. Scrum Master
3. Scrum Owner
4. Product Owner

Q: The Product Increment is a step toward a vision or goal. In which cases a Product Increment is valuable. Select all applicable

1. It reduces long-term maintenance costs
2. It increases customer satisfaction
3. It is developed with 25% low cost
4. It is delivered on time
5. It has all the features that the Product Owner expected

Q: A Product Backlog is visible to the Product Owner and stakeholders as they are the one who discuss on requirements to be implemented in product and Product Owner decides the order of Product Backlog Items. True or False

Q: Which statement best describes the Sprint Backlog? Select all applicable

1. Each task is estimated in days (half day, one day or maximum two days).
2. Every Sprint Backlog Item has a designated owner.
3. It is the Development Team's plan for the Sprint.
4. The Product Owner orders Product Backlog and Sprint Backlog.

Q: Alice a new developer has just joined the organization. She got allocated immediately on a Scrum project. She is curious on knowing how much time team should spend for Product Backlog Refinement?

1. As much as the Product Owner and Development Team think and they agree to create enough ready Product Backlog Items.
2. Up to 10% of the capacity of the Development Team.
3. As much as Product Owner thinks to create enough ready Product Backlog Items. Creating Product Backlog is the Product Owner's responsibility.
4. Up to 20% of the capacity of the Development Team.

Q: A Product Backlog is never complete. True or False

Q: Can the Product Owner invite stakeholders to Product Backlog Refinement sessions? Yes or No

Q: The purpose of a Sprint is to produce a Done Increment of Product. True or False.

Q: When should Scrum team members inspect Scrum artifacts and progress toward a Sprint Goal?

1. As frequently as possible
2. Frequently, but it should not get in the way of the work
3. At the Daily Scrum
4. At the Sprint Review

Q: What is the order of items in the Product Backlog?

1. The recently added items at the top
2. The recently added items at the bottom
3. The less clear items at the top so that discussion can happen
4. More valuable and most unclear items at the top
5. None of the above

Q: Who is allowed to change the Sprint Backlog during the Sprint?

1. The Scrum Master
2. The Development Team and the Product Owner
3. The Product Owner
4. The Development Team

Q: What is the Sprint Backlog?

1. The Product Backlog Items selected for this Sprint
2. The Product Backlog Items selected for next Sprint plus the plan for delivering them
3. The plan for delivering Product Backlog Items
4. None of the above

Q: The most applicable characteristics of the Product Owner from following are. Select all applicable.

1. Facilitator for task assignment
2. Product Value Maximizer

3. Lead Facilitator of Key Stakeholder Involvement
4. Product Marketplace Expert

Q: What are Product Backlog features? Select all applicable

1. As long as a product exists, its Product Backlog also exists
2. It is dynamic
3. It is a collection of features developed
4. It is never complete
5. It is a superset of Sprint Backlog

Q: Who all can make changes in the Product Backlog? Select all applicable

1. The Product Owner
2. The Key Stakeholders
3. The Scrum Master
4. The Development Team, but with permission of the Product Owner
5. Anyone in the organization

Q: Who is responsible for providing estimates for Product Backlog Items?

1. The Product Owner
2. The Development Team
3. The Scrum Master
4. COE Estimation Team
5. The Scrum Team, it's a collective responsibility

Q: Who creates the Increment?

1. The Scrum Team, it's a collective responsibility
2. The Development Team
3. Increment Integration Team
4. The Scrum Master
5. The Product Owner

Q: The Development Team may work with the Product Owner to remove or add work if they find that they have more or less capacity than anticipated. True or False

Q: Help yourself in finding out how the User Stories are ordered. Select all applicable

1. Risk, where safer User Stories are at the top, and riskier User Stories are at the bottom

2. Order is by first come first serve

3. Risk, where safer User Stories are at the bottom, and riskier User Stories are at the top

4. Size, where small User Stories are at the top, and large User Stories are at the bottom

5. User Stories are randomly arranged.

6. Whatever is deemed most appropriate by the Product Owner

Q: A new developer Vikram who has just joined Scrum team and the organization, wanted to know how should Development Team handle non-functional requirements and when should they incorporated? Help yourself in suggesting the best options to Vikram. Select all applicable

1. Non-functional requirements are more important than functional requirements hence should be implemented as soon as they are learned.

2. Non-functional requirements are less important than functional requirements hence should be implemented if Development Team has extra time.

3. Product Owner decides on whatever is most appropriate to the Product. Development Team Incorporate them into every Increment.

4. None of the above.

Q: What happens to the incomplete User Stories when the Sprint is over?

1. They were among the top priority hence were selected for the current Sprint, so they should be moved to the next Sprint Backlog.
2. They are moved back to the Product Backlog.
3. They should be re-estimated and moved back to the Product Backlog.
4. Sprint is not over until all User Stories are completed.

Q: The DEEP criteria are useful for determining if a Product Backlog has been structured in the right way. When is a Product Backlog Item "Ready" for selection in a Sprint Planning meeting?

1. When it meets the criteria in the Definition of "Ready."
2. When it meets the criteria in the Definition of Done.
3. When it meets both the criteria in the Definition of "Ready" and Definition of Done.
4. When it can be Done within one Sprint
5. When all tasks required for completing it are identified.

Q: Who should know the most about the advancement toward a business goal or a release, and be able to explain the alternative options most clearly?

1. The Product Owner
2. The Development Team
3. The Scrum Master
4. The Business Planner Team

Q: The Sprint Backlog is an ordered list of everything that might be needed in the product and is the only source of requirements for any modifications to the product. True or False

Q: How many weeks are required to release Increment for the Backlog that has 240 points, Sprint duration is 3 weeks, Velocity per Sprint is 45 points?

1. 12 weeks
2. 16 weeks
3. 6 weeks
4. 18 weeks

Q: a developer Kendall, asked Scrum Master Tom, how should a Product Backlog Item be refined before its development begins? Select two best options

1. In a manner that developers are clear enough
2. Developer should be identified who is responsible for developing item.
3. In a way that it can be Done in the time-boxed duration of one Sprint
4. All the tasks required for completing it should be identified before Sprint Planning meeting and each task should not take more than 2–3 days of efforts for implementation

Q: When should Product Increment be shipped? Select all applicable

1. When it makes sense
2. When the market is favorable for the product
3. After each Sprint
4. When the Increment is shippable
5. When the Development team and Product Owner feels so

Q: Technical Debt removal over time is important to the long-term viability of a product. Which of the following is a way of decreasing Technical Debt?

1. 50% functional and 50% non-functional requirements should be developed in each Sprint. Ignoring non-functional requirements increases Technical Debt

2. Improving the Definition of "Ready"

3. Improving the Definition of Done

4. Having one dedicated Sprint once in a quarter to clear the Technical Debt

Q: What is the advantage of using value points to order the Product Backlog?

1. There is no benefit. User Stories are recommended by Scrum Guide

2. Value is related to cost and Product Owner drives the project based on budget

3. Makes the ordering more transparent

4. Sprint Backlog uses value points for task estimation hence Product Backlog also uses value point

Q: The DEEP criteria are useful for determining if a Product Backlog has been structured in the right way. When should the Product Backlog Items be refined? Select two

1. In the Sprint 0 (also called as hardening Sprint)

2. During the Sprint, if they have not been refined in the previous Sprints

3. In one or two preceding Sprints

4. In the Sprint Review

5. In the time between the two Sprints

Q: Chrissy a new Scrum Master joined the Scrum Team which have executed 6 Sprint successfully. In one Scrum session, Chrissy said consistent Sprint Goals accomplishment is an indication that the team is becoming a high-performance team. Do you agree with Chrissy? Yes or No

Chapter 10

Artifact Transparency

Overview

Scrum relies on transparency. Decisions to optimize value and control risk are made based on the perceived state of the artifacts. To the extent that transparency is complete, these decisions have a sound basis. To the extent that the artifacts are incompletely transparent, these decisions can be flawed, the value may diminish, and risk may increase.

The Scrum Master must work with the Product Owner, Development Team, and other involved parties to understand if the artifacts are completely transparent. There are practices for coping with incomplete transparency; the Scrum Master must help everyone apply the most appropriate practices in the absence of complete transparency.

A Scrum Master can detect incomplete transparency by inspecting the artifacts, sensing patterns, listening carefully to what is being said, and detecting differences between expected and real results.

The Scrum Master's job is to work with the Scrum Team and the organization to increase the transparency of the artifacts. This work usually involves learning, convincing, and change. Transparency does not occur overnight but is a path.

Definition of Done

Definition of Done (DoD) is a checklist of the types of work that the team is expected to successfully complete before it can declare its work (Product Increment) to be potentially shippable. It is a list of conditions and expectations that Product Increment must met in order for it to be released into production. A Done Increment is required at the Sprint Review.

Table 10: A sample Definition of Done:

SN	Items
1	Code complete
2	Code peer reviewed
3	User Manual updated
4	All tests are automated
5	All web pages to load in 1 second
6	There must be no severity 1 defects
7	All acceptance criteria for the PBI must pass
8	Acceptance Tested
9	Product Owner reviewed and accepted

When a Product Backlog item or an Increment is described as Done, everyone must understand and have a shared understanding of what Done means i.e., all work is performed as listed in the definition of Done.

- All potentially releasable functionality adheres to the Scrum Team's current definition of Done, and Product Increment is releasable.

- The same definition guides the Development Team in knowing how many Product Backlog Items it can select during a Sprint Planning. DoD provides clarity on forecasting work deemed feasible for a Sprint.

- DoD is used to assess the work actually done compared to what was required to be done, DoD assess when work on Product Backlog Items, and the Product Increment is complete.

- DoD provides clarity on the progress of development throughout a Sprint.

- The content of the definition of Done should be self-explanatory and transparent. Transparency requires common standards, and the definition of Done sets the standard for releasable.

- If the definition of Done for an Increment is part of the conventions, standards or guidelines of the development organization, all Scrum Teams must follow it as a minimum. If Done for an Increment is not a convention of the development organization, the Development Team of the Scrum Team must define a definition of Done appropriate for the product.

- Primary ownership of the definition of Done lies with the Development Team. No one should force the Development Team to change the definition of Done. The DoD is for the whole Scrum Team. However, the Development Team is responsible for it, on behalf of the Scrum Team.

- As Scrum Teams mature, it is expected that their definitions of Done will expand to include more stringent criteria for higher quality. New definitions, as used, may uncover work to be done in previously Done increments. Any product or system should have a definition of Done that is a standard for any work done on it.

- A good definition of Done can help reduce technical debt. No adherence to the agreed definition of Done by the Development Team generally results in increased technical debt as it creates false assumptions about the actual state of the system.

- Nonfunctional requirements are added to the definition of Done so that team members can take care of them every Sprint.

- Security-related requirements could also be added to the definition of Done.

Definition of Done Vs Acceptance Criteria

The Definition of Done applies to the Product Increment. The Product Increment is composed of PBIs, so each Product Backlog Item must be completed in conformance with the work specified by the DoD checklist.

Each Product Backlog Item can have a set of conditions of satisfaction (Acceptance Criteria) specified by the Product Owner. Acceptance criteria are optional. Product Owner will verify these acceptance criteria while performing acceptance testing.

The Product Owner should guarantee that these acceptance criteria are developed before an item is accepted in Sprint Planning. The Development Team can pick up a PBI even if acceptance criteria are not specified, based on the Development Team and the Product Owner's mutual understanding.

Examples of DoD and Acceptance Criteria:

- Definition of Done

    o   No critical defects will be accepted

    o   Code coverage percentage should be at least 70%

    o   All web pages to load in under 2 seconds

- Acceptance Criteria

    o   The password must be no less than 8 and no greater than 12 characters, contain at least one uppercase letter, one lower case letter, and at least one number

    o   An error message should be displayed if the webpage is not responding

    o   An auto-generated email will be sent once the report is generated

A Product Backlog Item is considered done when acceptance criteria and the Definition of Done are met.

Done for Multiple Teams

Definition of Done must take into account the DoD of the other Scrum Teams working on the same product, to ensure there is uniformity in the quality of the different parts of the product.

When multiple Development Teams are working on a single product, they must agree on a common Definition of Done and can have their own Definition of Done as well. This common Definition of Done should enable their integrated increments to be potentially shippable. The Development Teams on all of the Scrum Teams must mutually define the definition of Done.

Table 11: Example for Definition of Done for three Scrum teams.

Teams	Items in Definition of Done
Team 1	DoD Item1, DoD Item2, DoD Item4
Team 2	DoD Item2, DoD Item3, DoD Item4, DoD Item5
Team 3	DoD Item1, DoD Item2, DoD Item4, DoD Item5

Common Definition of Done: DoD Item2, DoD Item4

In addition to the common Definition of Done, all teams must also adhere to their own Definitions of Done. For Example. Team 1 will complete DoD Item2, DoD Item4 for each PBI. However, team 1 is able to do DoD Item1 as per its done criteria.

Sample Questions

Q: Who is responsible for the creation of the Definition of Done?

1. Development Team
2. The Product Owner
3. The Scrum Master
4. The Scrum Team
5. Product Owner and Development Team

Q: Done indicates all work to create an Increment of software that is ready for integration testing. True or False.

Q: Sonu, a new developer who never worked on Agile projects has joined a new Scrum Team. Scrum Master Mohammed was explaining him about the purpose of having a Definition of Done from following options. Select all applicable.

1. It helps to calculate the velocity of the Scrum team
2. It tracks the percent completeness of a Product Backlog Item
3. Ensures artifact transparency
4. It controls whether the developers have performed their tasks
5. It guides the Development Team in creating a forecast at the Sprint Planning
6. None of the above

Q: Definition of Done should be fixed. True or False

Q: How a team knows when a Backlog Item is Done?

1. The Scrum Master says it is Done.
2. The Sprint time-box expires
3. The testers after doing a complete testing says it is done
4. None of the above

Q: When is the Sprint Backlog created?

1. As soon as possible
2. As soon as possible, it should not come in the work of Development Team
3. During the Sprint Planning meeting
4. During the Backlog Refinement meeting

Q: A Development Team has completed one project in the organization. They got opportunity to work on a new Scrum project. They wanted to create a Definition of Done. What should they take into account for the Definition of Done? Select all applicable

1. Conventions, standards, and guidelines of the Organization
2. Definition of Done of other Scrum Teams working on other products
3. As they are new, they should spend one Sprint on creating Definition of Done so that all can understand Scrum well before starting the development
4. Definition of Done of other Scrum Teams working on the same Product

Q: Should the Product Owner approve the Definition of Done? Yes or No

Q: A new Development Team in GathaCorp wanted to know how a Scrum project's deliverables are different than the regular Waterfall project deliverable. This Development Team has plan to work on a new Scrum project once they complete their current assignment. Which one of the following statements is right with respect to acceptance of any Scrum Project deliverables? Select all applicable

1. In Sprint Review meeting, Scrum managers sign off any particular deliverable post review of done increment

2. The team should get acceptance of project deliverables from the end users during a UAT phase at the end of the project

3. Acceptance of any particular deliverable on the project is gained from all stakeholders at the same time

4. None of the above

Q: Definition of Done is a checklist of the types of work that the team is expected to successfully complete before it can declare its work (Product Increment) to be potentially shippable. How does the Definition of Done help to the Scrum Team? Select all applicable

1. It guides how many Product Backlog Items the Development Team can select during a Sprint Planning

2. It is used to evaluate when work on the Product Increment is complete

3. It describes what it takes for an Increment to be ready for release

4. It makes the work inspected at the Sprint Review transparent

5. All of the above

Q: When a Product Backlog Item or an Increment is described as Done, everyone must understand and have a shared understanding of what Done means. How could the stakeholders know if a Product Backlog Item is Done?

1. They should ask the Development Team members

2. They should compare what was Done, against the Definition of Done established by the Scrum Team

3. They should ask the Product Owner

4. None of the above

Q: The Definition of Done applies to the Product Increment. The Product Increment is composed of PBIs, so each PBI must be completed in conformance with the work specified by the DoD checklist. What best describes the definition of Done when many Scrum teams are working on a product?

1. Each Development Team defines and uses its own.

2. All teams must use the same DoD.

3. Each Development Team uses its own but must make its definition clear to all other teams, so the differences are known.

4. All Development Teams must have a definition of Done that makes their combined work potentially releasable.

5. None of the above

Q: Emilia, a senior developer was explaining to junior developer Rihanna that non-functional requirements are essential because they may affect the overall architecture of a product rather than the individual modules. Rihanna asked could non-functional requirements be part of the Definition of Done. What do you think Emilia should answer? Yes or No

Q: Scrum Master Leonardo was explaining to Development Team that Definition of Done guides how many Product Backlog Items the Development Team can select during a Sprint Planning. One of the developer Christopher asks to Leonardo that how does DoD guide this? Help yourself in finding out what would Leonardo answer from the following. Select all applicable.

1. DoD is a list of conditions and expectations that Product Increment must met in order for it to be released into production. The DoD helps to specify the work required to complete a Product Backlog Item for the product. It thus enables developer's estimate how long it can take. The Development Team can better plan which PBIs can be finished in the next Sprint.

2. DoD is a checklist and contains estimation guidelines

3. Both 1 & 2

4. None of the above

Q: Non-functional requirements describe the experience of the user while doing the work such as speed, security, uptime, response time, or accuracy. The Product Owner adds the non-functional requirements to the DoD. True or False

Q: Development Team can add a new sub-task to a Product Backlog Item to ensure that the non-functional requirements for that specific Product Backlog Item are met. True or False

Q: The content of the definition of Done should be self-explanatory and transparent. Transparency requires common standards, and the definition of Done sets the standard for releasable. What should be considered for the definition of Done? Select all applicable.

1. Experience of the Scrum Master
2. Definition of Done of other Scrum Teams working on the same Product
3. Definition of Done of other Scrum Teams working on other products
4. Experience of the Product Owner
5. Conventions, standards, and guidelines of the Organization

Q: Definition of Done can be reviewed and adapted during each Sprint Retrospective. True or False?

Q: Definition of Done can be reviewed and adapted during each Sprint Review. True or False?

Q: If in the Sprint a Product Backlog Item is not finished, nobody is responsible for it except the developer who was working on it. True or False

Q: Who creates the Definition of Done? Select two

1. The Development Team, if the definition of Done for an Increment is not part of the standards or guidelines of the development organization

2. The development organization, if the definition of Done for an Increment is part of the standards or guidelines of the development organization

3. The Product Owner as he or she is responsible for product and it's acceptance criteria

4. Development Team should create an internal DoD Team who takes care of DoD creation. In addition, it is a good practice to rotate the developers in DoD Team

5. Scrum Master creates the definition of 'Done' if Development Team ask Scrum Master to do it

Chapter 11

Agile Coach

Overview

An Agile Coach is a Scrum Master who takes teams (one or many teams, usually many teams) beyond getting Agile practices up and running into their deliberate, self-initiated, and joyful pursuit of high performance.

Agile Coach needs many skills for a coach to understand their perseverance and pathway. However, the below-mentioned roles which Agile coach plays make a difference in making high performing teams.

- Facilitator

- Teacher

- Coach-Mentor

- Conflict Navigator

- Collaboration Conductor

- Problem Solver

Anyone can claim themselves as an Agile Coach when they perform the following:

- Kicked-off new Agile teams.

- Implanted in the team a desire or zeal to uphold Agile values and practices.

- Coached team members one-on-one in a way that they started feeling a change in themselves as a result of the coaching.

- Coached a complete team for collaboration that produces excellent results thereby making a huge impact on the business.

- Coached the Product Owner in a way that she feels a constructive & sustainable coaching relationship with you.

- Coached many stakeholders (internal and external) in a way that they support the team and start feeling like one team rather as stakeholders to just push teams in crisis.

- Focusing on business value delivery through coaching everyone involved in delivering that value.

- Letting the team find their way. Taking a problem to the team instead of solving yourself (as an Agile Coach) even if you know the answer. You are not the best person to solve the problem. You (Agile Coach) should raise the observation to the team and let them tell you the root cause of the problem and, how will they handle the critical situation.

- Ensuring that through your examples and your way of approaching the situations, the team learns how to use Agile and are able to see the values of Agile.

- Helping the teams to move through conflict and live with it if it is unsolvable.

- Not joining as a team member when the team interacts and makes the conversations. Just observing team's in action; help them make their interactions better by powerful observations and by asking powerful questions and You looking for the quality of the team's conversation and not the content.

- Showing disappointments, joy, and excitement when you are sure that you did it for them and not for you.

- Listening to the speaker entirely before you speak

Teaching

An Agile coach works as a teacher many times during a team's lifetime from inception until it becomes a high performing team. The organization comes to approaches Agile coach when they want to go to Agile.

You set the rules and teach them to the team. You teach practices (The practices are basic moves) and principles (The principles tell the "why" for each practice).

One useful model of mastering comes from martial arts with three stages of proficiency:

- Shu – Follow the rule

- Ha – Break the rule

- Ri – Be the rule

These stages also describe the Agile teams as their first practices and then get good at Agile.

The necessity of teaching a team can come at any time as team works and produces outcomes. You may need to teach any or many parts of Scrum framework whenever you feel that the team goes out of track. You need to teach enough for that moment in a way it to convey them the lesson, without impacting the teams' momentum.

Coaching

Do take this quote by Lyssa Adkins into account: "Coaching is not about giving advice, but about supporting people to come up with their own solutions. If you ask the right questions, they always will."

A coach helps each person take the next step on their Agile journey. A coach works with individuals, or groups and/or multiple teams, to help them identify and achieve their goals. It is assumed that the people being coached, whether they are an individual or a group of teams, already have the knowledge about how the goal can be achieved, and the Coach's role coach just makes them realize this by is to take them through a sequence line of questioning powerful questions to get them to articulate these steps. This entire exercise is done without the coach being influencing or giving his or her own opinion on the subject. Please note that a coach only needs to be an expert in coaching and not necessarily an expert in the subject.

- When you coach an Agile team, you simultaneously coach them at the individual level and whole team level.

- Sprint Start – Whole team coaching during Sprint Planning helps them get better at making shared commitments. Individual coaching takes a dip while the Sprint work begins as compared to whole team coaching.

- Mid Sprint – The coaching of the entire team is mostly dropped to allow the team to concentrate on the task. Team coaching only takes place if the coach decides to provide the greatest thoughts into the effect. Individuals bring in the problems and complaints to the coach expecting some solutions from the coach. But, Coach coaches individuals to become better Agilest and offer tools they can use to resolve their own problems. Mid Sprint is the perfect time for individual coaching but needs to ensure it is not making any negative impact on the Sprint Goal.

- Sprint End – Whole team coaching comes to the fore, particularly in the Retrospective where individuals learn how to learn from each other. Individual coaching tends to slow in the Retrospective as the coach addresses the issues of individuals at the entire team level.

- Coaching during Retrospective enables the team does more than creating a to-do list of enhancements. Alternatively, coach in a manner that enables employees to learn best from each other rather than just preparing action items.

Teaching Vs Coaching

Teaching is an art of explaining to be specifically articulating, something to someone who gets easily understood. If someone asks us a question and if we are really on form, we feel we should teach them. We react by giving them our answer – "here is the answer, and here is how I got to it." The person wanders off, their problem resolved, and the knowledge imparted.

Unlike teaching, Coaching differs slightly. Coaches give individuals the skills to solve the problem by themselves. Coaching requires discipline and practice. Rather than digging into the issue, coaches use a range of techniques (many of the times, powerful questions) to encourage the individual to think deeply and creatively to resolve the issue themselves. It solves their problem at hand and builds skills and confidence to make better decisions from thereon.

But, in the scenario of teaching, a person may come back to the teacher with similar problems in the future. The skill of the coach is to develop the individual, group, or teams to handle any situation, making the right decisions independently irrespective of the nature of the problem.

Mentoring

Unlike Coaching and teaching, mentoring is very different in its nature. A mentor is the one who:

- A mentor is generally an expert on the topic and offers the people with guidance and potentially some direction.

- Mentor provides guidance based on their knowledge and prior experiences.

- A Mentor shares their Agile experiences and ideas to the team so as to implement in a similar way as was did in the past by them.

- Mentoring transfers your Agile knowledge and experience to the team.

Coaching Vs Mentoring

In the Agile world, coaching and mentoring are wrapped up in the cumulative term coaching. The Agile coach involves both coaching and mentoring. Let us quickly take a look at both of these skills.

Coaching:

In a Development Team, where the team wants to get to Continuous Delivery, the Agile Coach may ask, "What steps need to be taken to get to that desired outcome?" It is assumed that the coachee has the knowledge and that they will be able to understand and articulate what needs to happen, in order for them to get closer to or even indeed achieve their goal.

Mentoring:

Team looking to get to Continuous Delivery, a team coach might say something as "We need to focus on our test automation strategy so that when we are releasing more frequently, we are confident that our software is reliable." – In a way providing the team a direction to head towards achieving the goal.

There is a distinction between coaching and mentoring. As an Agile Coach, one should not be hung up if we are giving advice (mentoring) to our teams or supporting people to come up with their own solutions (coaching). A healthy balance between asking powerful questions and providing guidance or direction based on previous experiences will ensure that teams move effectively towards meeting their set goals.

Facilitator

An Agile Coach many a time needs to play the role of facilitator during his/her career in order to ease the team to embark on to the Agile journey.

- The facilitator facilitates the Scrum process. A facilitator reminds the team on their common objectives; help them to understand their common goal. Keeps the team on track to achieving their goals. The facilitator does not tell the team what those common goals should be and let the team decide the common goals.

- The facilitator promotes collaboration. If there are issues for collaboration among the team, the facilitator helps the team gets to the root cause (for any issue) by asking probing questions and ensure that everyone is working in harmony and tandem.

- The facilitator must play a supportive role, encouraging everyone to commit to their best thought processes and practices. Facilitators help make things happen and help build strong teams.

- The facilitator helps team members to do their work themselves. The facilitator does not force anyone to do anything.

- A facilitator uses many techniques, such as asking powerful questions to help the team improve the project outcome.

Sample Questions

Q: In Hamsa SoftTech organization Scrum Master Anne, Product Owner Cheryl and a Development Team of 7 members are working on a product development. 5 Sprints are completed successfully and Sprint duration is 2 weeks. The Development Team is discussing design and architecture for one new feature. Four developers are with one design approach (Approach A) and the remaining four are with another design approach (Approach B). Initially, developers were having healthy disagreements and after some time argument got intense. There was no conclusion and developers were not able to decide which approach to select out of two. In this situation, who do you think is responsible for resolving the situation?

1. Anne
2. Cheryl
3. Development Team
4. HR Team
5. Senior Developers from other Scrum Teams in Hamsa

Q: The stakeholder Luis is investing $ 3 Mn for developing one product. He is eager to see the first release of the product. The Product Owner Zinedine and Luis are excited as they have seen the first ready Product Increment as per their expectations in the Sprint Review meeting. They have decided to launch the release in the market. Luis is expecting end-users will suggest changes once they see the first release and he wanted to invest his money carefully. Luis is asking to stop next upcoming Sprints so that Developers will be available for fixing the changes needed in the Increment. Zinedine is focusing on next Sprints and wants Development Team to select the next priority valuable User Stories to deliver more value in next Sprints. What do you think should be done in this situation? Select all applicable.

1. Luis's decision must be finalized (stop the next two Sprints) as he know the market condition better than the Zinedine.

2. Make Scrum Master available for fixing the changes. Continue the Sprints and Development Team should deliver more value by implementing next priority valuable User Stories

3. Continue the Sprints. Include the end-users' feedback in the Sprint Backlog so that the Development Team can fix the changes on priority in the Sprint in which they are working. This way, the stakeholder will also be happy as end-users' requests are taken on priority.

4. Continue the Sprints. Include the end-users' feedback in the Product Backlog.

Q: A Scrum team has 7 developers, a Scrum Master Sachin and a Product Owner Viola. Team has created Definition of Done and 10 Sprints were executed successfully. From 11th Sprint, Development Team was not completing peer reviews for the Selected Product Backlog Items (Peer review was part of the Definition of Done). Post discussion with Viola, they have decided to update the Definition of Done to remove regression testing. Few developers suggested they should discuss with Sachin as well for his opinion. What do you think Sachin should do when Development Team discuss with him? Select all applicable

1. Sachin should agree for changing the Definition of Done as both Development Team and Sachin are agreeing.

2. Sachin should disagree as peer reviews are must to improve the quality of the product.

3. Sachin should tell Development Team that Definition of Done is not his responsibility and Development Team can do whatever they want.

4. Sachin should ask Viola to include peer review in her acceptance criteria so that even if Development Team remove it from DoD, acceptance criteria will ensure to perform the peer review.

5. None of the above.

Chapter 12

Managing Products with Agility

Overview

When developing a product with Scrum, planning takes place at multiple levels. Kenneth Rubin has listed planning at multiple levels as following (Kenneth, 2015).

- Strategy Planning

- Portfolio Planning

- Product Planning

- Release Planning

- Sprint Planning

- Daily Scrum

Formally, Scrum defines only Sprint Planning and Daily Scrum.

Strategy Planning

Strategic Planning is an organization's process of defining its strategy and making decisions on allocating its resources to pursue this strategy.

Strategic Planning involves defining your company's direction and describing how you allocate budgets and resources. Managing portfolios involves analyzing investment choices that support the company. Together, they form the basis of a robust business strategy for producing company products and services, handling customers and using competitive tactics. Strategic planning is conceptually at a higher level than Portfolio Planning.

Strategic Planning is a systematic process that helps you set an ambition for your business' future and determine how best to achieve it. A Strategic Planning helps an organization do a better job, because a plan focuses the energy, resources, and time of everyone in the organization in the same direction. It provides focus and direction to move from plan to action.

Portfolio Planning

Portfolio is a collection of products (current or proposed) of your organization. Portfolio Planning is an activity for determining which products (Portfolio Backlog Items) needs to be developed for an organization. Portfolio Planning focuses on both new products and ongoing development products. Portfolio Planning determines whether to fund the product and decide the order of the product development.

Participants:

- Internal Stakeholders – they decides priority of product development

- Product Owners of individual products – they suggest on resource requirements of their respective products

- Optionally, Subject Matter Experts (Domain and technical experts) – they will help in identifying any technical limitations for developing the product

Inputs:

- New product ideas and its details like cost, duration, etc. identified during Product Planning.

- Ongoing products data like cost, duration, etc. for remaining work identified during Product Planning.

Outputs:

- Portfolio Backlog – ordered list of proposed products that are approved for development in future.

- Set of active products – List of products that are approved for immediate development and ongoing products that are approved to continue.

Product Planning

Product Planning activity determines what the next version of the product should be or determines the ideas for new product. Product vision with high-level scope, timeline and cost is identified without spending much time, as these details will be needed in Portfolio Planning for product funding approvals. A product roadmap with a sequence of incremental releases is created. Initial Product Backlog with usually large User Stories is created.

We should have enough understanding on what should be in first release of the product (new product or next version of the ongoing product). Product Planning is at a higher level than Release Planning.

Participants:

- The Product Owner.

- Optionally, internal stakeholders.

- Optionally, Domain, Technical and market research experts.

- Optionally, the Scrum Master and the Development Team. Usually Scrum Master and Development are allocated to project if funding is approved in Portfolio Planning for immediate product development. Hence, Scrum team may not exist during initial Product Planning.

Inputs:

- Ideas for new product or next version of the ongoing product.

- Planning horizon – how far into the future we should consider when we are planning.

- Expected completion date for the Product Planning activities.

- Quantity and type of resources available to conduct Product Planning.

- Confidence threshold – the information that the decision makers need to make funding decision for product development.

Outputs:

- Product vision

- Initial Product Backlog (User Stories, usually at high level)

- Product roadmap with the incremental releases

- Confidence threshold artifacts that the decision makers need

Release Planning

Release Planning is done after Product Level Planning. Product roadmap has series of releases and a release on the product roadmap corresponds to a set of features in the Product Backlog. Release Planning creates the release plan (contains one or more Sprints) to determine which all features from Product Backlog (User Stories) will be delivered in next release and minimum releasable features are identified. Usually, Release Planning duration is one day or two (it is not mandatory, may vary).

In Release Planning activity scope, schedule and budget is reviewed and changes are made as needed. Product Backlog grooming also takes place as part of Release Planning. During Release Planning a

Sprint map (very high-level mapping of Product Backlog Items with Sprints) is created, though in Sprint Planning the Development Team and Product Owner decide which all Product Backlog Items to work on in that Sprint.

Release plans can be revised as part of each Sprint Review.

Participants:

- Stakeholders

- Scrum Team

Inputs:

- Product vision

- High-level Product Backlog

- Product roadmap

- Velocity of the team. For an existing team, we use the team's known velocity; otherwise, we forecast the team's velocity during release planning.

Outputs:

- Series of Sprints

- Updated Product Backlog

- Minimum releasable features

- Sprint Map

- Schedule and cost

Sample Questions

Note: There are no questions on this chapter as formally Scrum defines only Sprint Planning and Daily Scrum.

Appendix

For reader's convenience, the Evidence-Based Management and Nexus guides are printed under this appendix. The intention is only to ease the additional readings, which ignites the further deep diving in Scrum scaling and understanding business agility, being captured from one place instead of referring various other sources.

1. Evidence-Based Management (EBM)

Overview

I am adding here the content of Evidence-Based Management from Evidence-Based Management Guide. Scrum.Org. January 2019.

Organizations adopting Agile can easily lose sight of their real goal of improving the value they deliver, by focusing on improving activities and outputs instead of on business outcomes.

The whole point of adopting Agile is to improve business performance. When organizations lose sight of this, managers ask questions that seem sensible, but might create unintended and undesirable consequences. Some examples of such questions are:

- Is team velocity increasing?
- What is the quality level of code?
- How frequently are developers integrating code?

While the answers to these questions are interesting, they do not help an organization improve the value it delivers, or its ability to deliver value. Monitoring only the direct use of practices does not provide the best evidence of their effectiveness; for example, tracking a Development Team's velocity says nothing about whether that team is actually delivering something that is useful to customers or users.

Without measuring value, the success of any Agile initiative is based on nothing more than intuition and assumption. In contrast, the EBM approach measures value delivered as evidence of organizational agility, and provides ways to measure and improve the ability to deliver value. This approach enables organizations to make rational, fact-based decisions, elevating conversations from preferences and opinions to empirical evidence, logic, and insight.

EBM is an empirical approach that provides organizations with the ability to measure the value they deliver to customers and the means by which they deliver that value, and to use those measures to guide improvements in both.

EBM consists of four Key Value Areas (KVAs):

- Current Value

- Time-to-Market

- Ability to Innovate

- Unrealized Value

Each KVA focuses on a different aspect of either value, or the ability of the organization to deliver Value. Organizations without strength in all four KVAs may deliver short-term value, but will not be able to sustain it. Delivering value, happy stakeholders, and satisfied employees (Current Value) are important, but organizations must also show that they can meet market demand with timely delivery (Time-to-Market) while being able to sustain innovation over time (Ability to Innovate). Continued investment in the product is justified based on measures of as-yet (Unrealized Value) that could be realized if the product possessed the right capabilities.

Metrics are just one part in building a team's culture. They give quantitative insight into the team's performance and provide measurable goals for the team. While they are important, do not get obsessed. Listening to the team's feedback during Retrospectives is equally important in growing trust across the team, quality in the product, and development speed through the release process. Use both the quantitative and qualitative feedback to drive change.

Current Value (CV)

Reveals the value that the product delivers to customers, today. The goal of looking at CV is to maximize the value that an organization delivers to customers and stakeholders at the present time; it considers only what exists right now, not the value that might exist in the future. Questions that organizations need to continually re-evaluate for current value are:

1. How happy are users and customers today? Is their happiness improving or declining?

2. How happy are your employees? Is their happiness improving or declining?

3. How happy are your investors and other stakeholders? Is their happiness improving or declining?

A variety of things can improve CV: improving usability, improving customer or user outcomes, even creating a happier workplace. Looking at CV from the perspectives of customers or users, as well as investors, is obvious, but considering employee attitudes recognizes that employees are ultimately the producers of value. Engaged employees that know how to maintain, sustain and enhance are one of the most significant assets of an organization, and happy employees are more productive.

Example of Key Value Measures (KVMs):

- Revenue per Employee: The ratio (gross revenue/# of employees) is a key competitive indicator within an industry. This varies significantly by industry.

- Product Cost Ratio: Total expenses and costs for the product(s)/ system(s) being measured, including operational costs compared to revenue.

- Employee Satisfaction: It is the sentiment analysis to gauge employee engagement, energy and enthusiasm. Use employee satisfaction to find out how happy employees are. Are people happy about the way things are working? If your velocity is going up and happiness is going down, you are going to crash and burn, right? What you want is to keep happiness very high and velocity improving.

- Customer Satisfaction: Using a consistent customer satisfaction metric and measuring it for every release indicates whether the Scrum team is meeting its end goal – to provide value to customers. It is the sentiment analysis to gauge customer engagement and happiness with product. Find if users would recommend the software to others, do nothing, or recommend against it.

- Customer Usage Index: – Measurement of usage, find the degree to which customers find the product useful and whether actual usage meets expectations.

Time-to-Market (T2M)

Expresses the organization's ability to quickly deliver new capabilities, services, or products.

The goal of looking at Time-to-Market is to minimize the amount of time it takes for the organization to deliver value. Without actively managing Time-to-Market, the ability to sustainably deliver value in the future is unknown. Questions that organizations need to continually re-evaluate for time to market are:

1. How fast can the organization learn from new experiments?

2. How fast can you learn from new information and adapt?

3. How fast can you deliver new value to customers?

A variety of things can reduce the Time-to-Market: everything from removing internal communication bottlenecks to improving delivery pipeline automation to improving application maintainability and removing technical debt; anything that reduces time spent waiting or time spent performing work.

Example of KVMs:

- Build and integration frequency: The number of integrated and tested builds per time period. For a team that is releasing frequently or continuously, this measure is superseded by actual release measures.

- Release Frequency: The number of releases per time period, e.g. continuously, daily, weekly, monthly, quarterly, etc. This helps reflect the time needed to satisfy the customer with new and competitive products. At the end of each Sprint, the team should release software out to production. How often is that actually happening? Are most release builds getting shipped?

- Release Stabilization Period: The time spent correcting product problems between the point the developers say it is ready to release and the point where it is actually released to customers. This helps represent the impact of poor development practices and underlying design and code base.

- Mean Time to Repair: The average amount of time it takes from when an error is detected and when it is fixed. This helps reveal the efficiency of an organization to fix an error.

- Cycle Time: The amount of time from when work starts on a release until the point where it is actually released. This measure helps reflect an organization's ability to reach its customer.

- Lead Time: The amount of time from when an idea is proposed or a hypothesis is formed until a customer can benefit from that idea. This measure may vary based on customer and product. It is a contributing factor for customer satisfaction.

- Time-to-Learn: The total time needed to sketch an idea or improvement, build it, deliver it to users, and learn from their usage.

Ability to Innovate (A2I)

Expresses the ability of a product development organization to deliver new capabilities that might better meet customer needs.

The goal of looking at the A2I is to maximize the organization's ability to deliver new capabilities and innovative solutions. Organizations should continually re-evaluate their A2I by asking:

1. What prevents the organization from delivering new value?

2. What prevents customers or users from benefiting from that innovation?

A variety of things can impede a team from being able to deliver new capabilities and value:

Spending too much time fixing defects or reducing technical debt, having to maintain multiple code branches or product versions, a complex or monolithic application architecture, insufficient product-like environments to test on, lack of operational excellence, poor code management practices, lack of decentralized decision-making, inability to hire and inspire talented, passionate team-members, and so on.

As low-value features and systemic impediments accumulate, more budget and time is consumed maintaining the product or overcoming impediments, reducing its available capacity to innovate. In addition, anything that prevents users or customers from benefitting from innovation, such as hard to install software or lack of capabilities that would be compelling enough to warrant installing the software, will also reduce A2I.

Example of KVMs:

- Feature Usage Index: Measurement of features in the product that are frequently used. This helps capture features that are rarely or never used.

- Innovation Rate: The percentage of effort or cost spent on new product capabilities, divided by total product effort or cost. This provides insight into the capacity of the organization to deliver new product capabilities.

- Defect trends: Measurement of change in defects since last measurement. A defect is anything that reduces the value of the product to a customer, user, or to the organization itself. Defects are generally things that do not work as intended.

- On-Product Index: The percentage of time teams spend working on product and value.

- Installed Version Index: The number of versions of a product that are currently being supported. This reflects the effort the organization spends supporting and maintaining older versions of software.

- Technical Debt: A concept in programming that reflects the extra development and testing work that arises when "quick and dirty" solutions result in later remediation. It creates an undesirable impact on the delivery of value and an avoidable increase in waste and risk. Evaluate this metric to remove technical debt and waste around unfinished Sprint work.

- Production Incident Trends: The number of times the Development Team was interrupted to fix a problem in an installed product. The number and frequency of Production Incidents can help indicate the stability of the product.

- Active code branches, time spent merging code between branches: These measures are like the Installed Version Index, since different deployed versions usually have separate code branches.

- Time spent context switching: Number of meetings per day per person, and the number of times a day team members are interrupted to help people outside the team can give simple insight into the magnitude of the problem.

Unrealized Value (UV)

Suggests the potential future value that could be realized if the organization could perfectly meet the needs of all potential customers.

The goal of looking at Unrealized Value is for the organization to maximize the value that it realizes from the product over time. Questions that organizations need to continually re-evaluate for unrealized value are:

1. Can any additional value be created for our organization in this market or other markets?

2. Is it worth the effort and risk to pursue these untapped opportunities?

3. Should further investments be made to capture additional Unrealized Value?

These questions cannot be completely answered in isolation from the UV of other products; the decision to invest in one product means not investing in others. Considering both CV and UV provides organizations with a way to balance present and possible future benefits.

Example of KVMs:

- Market Share: The relative percentage of the market controlled by the product.

- Customer or user satisfaction gap: It can be measured as the difference between a customer's desired experience and their current experience. Use this metric to maximize the value that the organization realizes from a product over time.

How to Use Key Value Measures

Just starting to measure KVAs can drive some improvement, because it will show you immediately where you have improvement opportunities. Using a more systematic approach can provide even better results by enabling organizations to continuously learn and improve the value derived from software investments. To produce genuine and long lasting improvements, establish a learning loop as outlined below.

1. Quantify Value: The first step in the EBM learning loop is to quantify value in the form of KVM's. The process of defining and aligning around KVM's itself might be valuable to an organization, because it can create transparency around what is being optimized.

2. Measure KVMs: The next step in the EBM learning loop is to establish initial values or a baseline measure for the KVMs of interest. This step provides an initial view of the viability of the product and the ability of the organization to deliver the product. It creates transparency around relative strengths and weaknesses.

3. Select KVAs to improve: With a clear view of current organizational value and an understanding of the measures that reveal it, managers of software organizations can now make informed decisions about which KVAs would be most valuable to change. Do not try to affect too many KVAs within a single learning loop. Making small incremental changes and then quickly measuring the result is better than delaying improvement and measurement by changing too many factors at once. Changing many factors at the same time can also pose challenges when trying to establish causality between outcomes and activities. Short cycles with few changes are the most effective way to make sustainable improvements to an organization's overall agility.

4. Conduct practice experiments to improve targeted KVAs: After choosing a desired KVA to improve, select, at most, a few practices that you think will improve the associated KVM(s), and run an experiment. For example, a software organization that wants to increase quality might choose to focus on reducing the Defects KVM. They may decide to try implementing test-first practices to increase the test coverage and the quality focus of the Development Teams.

5. Evaluate results: Once the results of the experiment are measured, they should be compared with the KVM values before the changes were made. If the experiment produced improved measured, the change is kept, otherwise other improvements are tried. The learning loop continues until the KVA reflect the desired results.

It is very important to understand that Scrum metrics focus on predictable software delivery, making sure Scrum teams deliver maximum value to customers with every iteration. Use the measures to guide the improvements. Management should not misuse these metrics for their own purposes.

Sample Questions

Q: In Colossi Mutual Globals, a Development Team of 7 members, Scrum Master Johann and Product Owner Raphael are working on a Scrum project with two weeks Sprint duration. Eleven Sprints completed successfully. While working, Development Team members gained the good domain knowledge and were able to understand business needs and goals. They were also able to share new ideas with Raphael and stakeholders. Because of some emergency, the Raphael decided to go on leave without pay for 2 years. A new Product Owner Gottfried joins the organization. As Scrum Team needed a Product Owner, Gottfried has been asked to join the team immediately without getting full details related to his responsibilities. Considering this situation, Johann advice Gottfried on following. Select all applicable

1. Attend the Daily Scrum, interact with developers and get the status of daily development activities directly from each developer. Developers will feel connected with you.
2. Do not take any leaves for 3–4 Sprints.
3. Initially, trust developers and stakeholders for adding requirements to the Product Backlog. Interaction with them will help you to understand the product quickly.
4. As the Development Team is matured than you, it is good to get initial knowledge transfer from the Development Team and then provide your inputs.

Q: A new Product Owner Nelson has joined the new organization. Nelson wanted to know the metrics that will help him to determine that value is being delivered. Help yourself in selecting two metrics from following.

1. Customer Satisfaction
2. Team Velocity
3. Capacity

4. Time to Market

5. Productivity

Q: A startup organization JapaCorp which never worked in Agile earlier has decided to adopt Scrum. Management committee of JapaCorp wants to know how would their organization know that a product built through Scrum is successful? Select suitable options from following.

1. By measuring the actual time versus the time estimated for development

2. By measuring that velocity has increased since the last release

3. By releasing often, and updating Key Performance Indicators (KPIs) on value after every release and feeding this information back into work on the Product Backlog

4. By the Product Owner and stakeholders accepting the Increment at the Sprint Review

5. By comparing time to market since last release that is improved by 50%

Q: The following metrics are mandated by Scrum to track Sprint progress.

1. Burnup chart

2. Burndown chart

3. Team Velocity

4. All of the above

5. Both 2&3

6. None of above

Q: Michelle is a Manager in Tattva Globals, she is the supervisor of a 7 developers who are working on a Scrum project. The Development Team is working Michelle from the last 1 year, and she trust their decisions. Now, Development Team feels they need one more developer to increase their capacity, as their need is to deliver more features and value to the customer from next Sprint onwards. They ask Michelle to increase one developer. Michelle do not have any budget constraint for this request. What should Michelle do? Select all applicable

1. Ask Development Team to wait for next 5–6 Sprints and get back to her if they feel the need of additional developer at that time

2. Michelle share her budgetary amount of $100K (per year) for this new developer with Development Team. Ask Development Team to connect with HR department and onboard the new developer

3. Michelle asks Development Team not to contact her directly, share your requirements with Scrum Master and she will discuss with Scrum Master

4. Michelle finalize one new developer with the help of Development Team for evaluation

5. Michelle contacts other Scrum teams in Tattva to see if there are any developers who are free and can be allocated for this project

Q: Joseph is a portfolio Manager in Kevala Global Soft. Every financial year, Joseph creates business plan for product development in Kevala for the entire year and keep on revisiting it as needed. This year, he needs to create a delivery plan for an in-process Scrum product for next twelve months. Four Scrum Teams are working on this product. Which of the following statement is true. Select all applicable

1. Work with Product Owner to get the forecast
2. Ask Scrum Master to do this activity on behalf of him
3. Work with Development Teams to get the forecast
4. As this is a Scrum product, planning is not needed in Agile
5. Joseph can create his plan with historical data

Q: Which of the following statement is true about an Agile project. Select all applicable

1. As many number of deliveries on short notice as Agile business needs
2. Get something occasional early released as quickly as possible
3. A regular pattern of delivery of developer-focused products
4. A regular pattern of delivery of business-valued increments
5. Agile means daily integration and continuous delivery on daily basis

Q: Agile methods are described as Adaptive because the progress rate of an Agile project is continually reviewed to allow adaptation. True or False

Q: Agile methods are described as Adaptive because Agile teams have the ability to respond to frequent changes and to learn on a project by changing the plan. True or False

Q: In an Agile training session, debate was going on whether Managers are required or not in Agile projects. An Engineer Aryabhata said Project Managers are not needed in Agile because teams are self-organizing. Do you agree with Aryabhata? True or False

Q: Which of the following statement is true about a Scrum approach. Select all applicable

1. Occasional early deliveries, if the organization is willing to accept slightly lower quality
2. Get something business-valuable delivered as quickly as possible, consistent with the right level of quality
3. Get something developer focused delivered as quickly as possible, consistent with the right level of quality
4. Get working product of the right quality, early and incrementally
5. Get something delivered early with no documentation

Q: Agile product is almost as good in quality as a Waterfall development and Agile approach to team working is Agile team should not strive for a sustainable pace and a normal working week. True or False

Q: The Agile team develops product of a professional quality which fits the business need and should expect to work longer hours towards the end of the Sprint to deliver all that was committed. True or False

Q: A startup organization wanted to implement Agile across the organization. A senior manager Kaliya said an Agile customer needs a thorough knowledge of Agile methods for Agile to work. Do you agree with Kaliya? Yes or No

Q: How will you describe an Agile team? Select all applicable

1. Is self-organizing, with each member having the equal technical skills and never take help from other teams in the organization
2. Collaborates and supports its team members
3. Ensures that weak members of the team are allocated the less complicated tasks
4. Courageous to change and adapt
5. Composed of 70% seniors and 30% juniors

Q: A small software development company decided to adopt Agile. In a board members meeting, one of the senior most business leader wanted to know about the Agile process. Help yourself in selecting one of the following.

1. Encourages the Agile team to meet regularly
2. Has fixed number of meetings and cannot have any additional meetings
3. Recommends review of Agile artifacts on daily basis
4. Encourages the Agile team to work overtime to achieve the committed work

Q: A senior developer Hafpor said, no one tells the Development Team how to turn Product Backlog into Increments of potentially releasable functionality. How would you describe a self-organizing Development Team with respect to Sprint Backlog from the following statements? Select all applicable

1. Technical or domain experts external to the team can attend the Sprint Planning meeting. Hence, the Development Team invites them to the Sprint Planning to help them create a complete Sprint Backlog.

2. Definition of Done is a checklist of the types of work that the Development Team is expected to complete before it can declare Product Increment to be potentially shippable. Development Team creates its Sprint Backlog to reflect all work that is part of the definition of Done.

3. Sprint Backlog is mandatory artifact and Scrum Master drafts initial version of Sprint Backlog based on his or her experience and gives it to Development Team. Development Team updates it during Sprint Planning and as needed.

4. If the Development Team is self-organized, they do not have to spend time on creating Sprint Backlog and can utilize that time for product development.

Q: The Agile leader directs the work of the Development Team only if they are inexperienced, experienced team is self-organized, collaborate, and manage their work. True or False

Q: A new developer Jill feels the Development Team should not be involved in their work-allocation otherwise senior developers will always select simple task and juniors will have to work on complicated task. Do you agree with Jill? Yes or No

Q: Select true statements from following on Agile approach to documentation. Select all applicable

1. Priority is potentially shippable increment hence do documentation if time is available

2. Do enough documentation for a change from coding work

3. Do the necessary documentation to support the development and use of the product

4. It is a myth that Agile says no documentation, in fact increments are of short duration hence all developers are busy in their assigned work hence cannot spend more time on knowledge sharing with developers so more documentation is needed in Agile

Q: How would you describe the working culture of an Agile team?

1. Cooperative

2. Collaborative

3. Directive

4. Technical

5. Introspective

Q: How would you describe the leadership style of an Agile Leader?

1. Directive

2. Assertive

3. Incremental

4. Facilitative

5. Iterative

Q: Which of the following are attributes of an Agile team?

1. Trust of fellow team members to do the work

2. Responsiveness to change

3. Believe in professional work and do not trust anyone

4. None of the above

Q: Select true statements from following about project planning. Select all applicable

1. It is normal to need to plan and re-plan as the project progresses

2. If you plan and re-plan multiple times as the project progresses, results will not be delivered on time

3. Scrum Master can spend time on planning as he is not involved in development

4. Plans are not required as Agile is incremental and iterative

2. Nexus in Detail

Overview

Scaling concepts must be clear if you want to achieve an advanced level in Scrum. I am adding here the content of Nexus from the Nexus Guide. Schwaber, Ken and Scrum.org developed Nexus. The Nexus Guide is written and provided by Schwaber, Ken and Scrum.Org. January 2018.

Purpose of the Nexus Guide

Nexus is a framework for developing and sustaining scaled product and software delivery initiatives. It uses Scrum as its building block.

Definition of Nexus

Nexus (n): a relationship or connection between people or things.

Nexus is a framework consisting of roles, events, artifacts, and rules that bind and weave together the work of approximately three to nine Scrum Teams working on a single Product Backlog to build an Integrated Increment that meets a goal.

Nexus Background

Software delivery is complex, and the integration of that work into working software has many artifacts and activities that must be coordinated to create a Done outcome. The work must be organized and sequenced, the dependencies resolved, and the outcomes staged.

Many developers have used the Scrum framework to work collectively to develop and deliver an Increment of working software. However, if more than one Scrum Team is working off the same Product Backlog and in the same codebase for a product, difficulties often arise. If the developers are not on the same collocated team, how will they communicate when they are doing work that will affect each other? If they work on different teams, how will they integrate their work and test the Integrated Increment? These challenges appear when two Scrum Teams are integrating their work into a single Increment, and become significantly more difficult when three or more Scrum Teams integrate their work into a single Increment.

There are many dependencies that arise between the work of multiple teams that collaborate to create a complete and Done Increment at least once every Sprint. These dependencies are related to

1. Requirements: The scope of the requirements may overlap, and the manner in which they are implemented may also affect each other. That knowledge should be considered when ordering the Product Backlog and selecting Product Backlog Items.

2. Domain knowledge: The people on the teams have knowledge of various business and computer systems. Their knowledge should be distributed across the Scrum Teams to ensure that the teams have the knowledge they need to do their work, to minimize interruptions between Scrum Teams during a Sprint.

3. Software and test artifacts: The requirements are, or will be, instantiated in software.

To the extent that requirements, team members' knowledge, and software artifacts are mapped to the same Scrum Teams, teams can reduce the number of dependencies between them.

When software delivery using Scrum is scaled, these dependencies of requirements, domain knowledge, and software artifacts should drive the organization of the Development Teams. To the extent that it does, productivity will be optimized.

Nexus Framework

Nexus is a process framework for multiple Scrum Teams working together to create an Integrated Increment. Nexus is consistent with Scrum and its parts will be familiar to those who have used Scrum.

The difference is that more attention is paid to dependencies and interoperation between Scrum Teams, delivering at least one Done Integrated Increment every Sprint.

Nexus consists of:

- Roles: A new role, the Nexus Integration Team, exists to coordinate, coach, and supervise the application of Nexus and the operation of Scrum so the best outcomes are derived. The Nexus Integration Team consists of the Product Owner, a Scrum Master, and Nexus Integration Team Members.

- Artifacts: All Scrum Teams use the same, single Product Backlog. As the Product Backlog Items are refined and made ready, indicators of which team will do the work inside a Sprint are made transparent. A new artifact, the Nexus Sprint Backlog, exists to assist with transparency during the Sprint. All Scrum Teams maintain their individual Sprint Backlogs.

- Events: Events are appended to, placed around, or replace (in the case of the Sprint Review) regular Scrum events to augment them. As modified, they serve both the overall effort of all Scrum Teams in the Nexus, and each individual team.

Nexus Process Flow

A Nexus consists of multiple cross-functional Scrum Teams working together to deliver a potentially releasable Integrated Increment at least by the end of each Sprint. Based on dependencies, the teams may self-organize and select the most appropriate members to do specific work.

- Refine the Product Backlog: The Product Backlog needs to be decomposed so that dependencies are identified and removed or minimized. Product Backlog Items are refined into thinly sliced pieces of functionality and the team likely to do the work should be identified.

- Nexus Sprint Planning: Appropriate representatives from each Scrum Team meet to discuss and review the refined Product Backlog. They select Product Backlog Items for each team. Each Scrum Team then plans its own Sprint, interacting with other teams as appropriate. The outcome is a set of Sprint Goals that align with the overarching Nexus Sprint Goal, each Scrum Team's Sprint Backlog and a single Nexus Sprint Backlog. The Nexus Sprint Backlog makes the work of all Scrum Team's selected Product Backlog Items and any dependencies transparent.

- Development work: All teams frequently integrate their work into a common environment that can be tested to ensure that the integration is done.

- Nexus Daily Scrum: Appropriate representatives from each Development Team meet daily to identify if any integration issues exist. If identified, this information is transferred back to each Scrum Team's Daily Scrum. Scrum Teams then use their Daily Scrum to create a plan for the day, being sure to address the integration issues raised during the Nexus Daily Scrum.

- Nexus Sprint Review: The Nexus Sprint Review is held at the end of the Sprint to provide feedback on the Integrated Increment that a Nexus has built over the Sprint. All individual Scrum Teams meet with stakeholders to review the Integrated Increment. Adjustments may be made to the Product Backlog.

- Nexus Sprint Retrospective: Appropriate representatives from each Scrum Team meet to identify shared challenges. Then, each Scrum Team holds individual Sprint Retrospectives. Appropriate representatives from each team meet again to discuss any actions needed based on shared challenges to provide bottom-up intelligence.

Nexus Roles

Nexus roles, events, and artifacts inherit the purpose and intent attributes of the corresponding Scrum roles, events, and artifacts, as documented in the Scrum Guide.

A Nexus consists of a Nexus Integration Team and approximately three to nine Scrum Teams.

Nexus Integration Team

The Nexus Integration Team is accountable for ensuring that a Done Integrated Increment (the combined work completed by a Nexus) is produced at least once every Sprint. The Scrum Teams are responsible for delivering Done Increments of potentially releasable products, as prescribed in Scrum. All roles for members of the Scrum Teams are prescribed in the Scrum Guide.

The Nexus Integration Team consists of:

- The Product Owner

- A Scrum Master

- One or more Nexus Integration Team Members

Members of the Nexus Integration Team are often also members of the individual Scrum Teams in that Nexus. If this is the case, they must give priority to their work on the Nexus Integration Team; membership in the Nexus Integration Team takes precedence over individual Scrum Team membership. This preference helps ensure that the work to resolve issues affecting many teams has priority.

Composition of the Nexus Integration Team may change over time to reflect the current needs of a Nexus. Common activities the Nexus Integration Team might perform include coaching, consulting, and highlighting awareness of dependencies and cross-team issues. It might also perform work from the Product Backlog.

The Scrum Teams address integration issues within the Nexus. The Nexus Integration Team provides a focal point of integration for the Nexus. Integration includes resolving any technical and non-technical cross-team constraints that may impede a Nexus' ability to deliver a constantly Integrated Increment. They should use bottom-up intelligence from the Nexus to achieve resolution.

Product Owner in the Nexus Integration Team

A Nexus works off a single Product Backlog, and as described in the Scrum framework, a Product Backlog has a single Product Owner who has the final say on its contents. The Product Owner is responsible for maximizing the value of the product and the work performed and integrated by the Scrum Teams in a Nexus. The Product Owner is a member of the Nexus Integration Team.

The Product Owner is accountable for managing the Product Backlog so that maximum value is derived from the Integrated Increment created by a Nexus. How this is done may vary widely across organizations, Nexuses, Scrum Teams, and individuals.

Scrum Master in the Nexus Integration Team

The Scrum Master in the Nexus Integration Team has overall responsibility for ensuring the Nexus framework is understood and enacted. This Scrum Master may also be a Scrum Master in one or more of the Scrum Teams in that Nexus.

Nexus Integration Team Members

The Nexus Integration Team consists of professionals who are skilled in the use of tools, various practices, and the general field of systems engineering. Nexus Integration Team Members ensure the Scrum Teams within the Nexus understand and implement the practices and tools needed to detect dependencies, and frequently integrate all artifacts to the definition of Done. Nexus Integration Team Members are responsible for coaching and guiding the Scrum Teams in a Nexus to acquire, implement, and learn these practices and tools.

Additionally, the Nexus Integration Team coaches the individual Scrum Teams on the necessary development, infrastructural, or architectural standards required by the organization to ensure the development of quality Integrated Increments.

If their primary responsibility is satisfied, Nexus Integration Team Members may also work as Development Team members in one or more Scrum Teams.

Nexus Events

The duration of Nexus events is guided by the length of the corresponding events in the Scrum Guide. They are time-boxes in addition to their corresponding Scrum events.

Refinement

Refinement of the Product Backlog at scale serves a dual purpose. It helps the Scrum Teams forecast which team will deliver which Product Backlog Items, and it identifies dependencies across those teams. This transparency allows the teams to monitor and minimize dependencies.

Refinement of Product Backlog Items by the Nexus continues until the Product Backlog Items are sufficiently independent to be worked on by a single Scrum Team without excessive conflict.

The number, frequency, duration and attendance of Refinement is based on the dependencies and uncertainty inherent in the Product Backlog. Product Backlog Items pass through different levels of decomposition from very large and vague requests to actionable work that a single Scrum Team could deliver inside a Sprint.

Refinement is continuous throughout the Sprint as necessary and appropriate. Product Backlog refinement will continue within each Scrum Team in order for the Product Backlog Items to be ready for selection in a Nexus Sprint Planning event.

Nexus Sprint Planning

The purpose of Nexus Sprint Planning is to coordinate the activities of all Scrum Teams in a Nexus for a single Sprint. The Product Owner provides domain knowledge and guides selection and priority decisions. The Product Backlog should be adequately refined with dependencies identified and removed or minimized prior to Nexus Sprint Planning.

During Nexus Sprint Planning, appropriate representatives from each Scrum Team validate and make adjustments to the ordering of the work as created during Refinement events. All members of the Scrum Teams should participate to minimize communication issues.

The Product Owner discusses the Nexus Sprint Goal during Nexus Sprint Planning. The Nexus Sprint Goal describes the purpose that will be achieved by the Scrum Teams during the Sprint. Once the overall work for the Nexus is understood, Nexus Sprint Planning continues with each Scrum Team performing their own separate Sprint Planning. The Scrum Teams should continue to share newly found dependencies with other Scrum Teams in the Nexus. Nexus Sprint Planning is complete when each Scrum Team has finished their individual Sprint Planning events.

New dependencies may emerge during Nexus Sprint Planning. They should be made transparent and minimized. The sequence of work across teams may also be adjusted. An adequately refined Product Backlog will minimize the emergence of new dependencies during Nexus Sprint Planning. All Product Backlog Items selected for the Sprint and their dependencies should be made transparent on the Nexus Sprint Backlog.

Nexus Sprint Goal

The Nexus Sprint Goal is an objective set for the Sprint. It is the sum of all the work and Sprint Goals of the Scrum Teams within the Nexus. The Nexus should demonstrate the functionality that it has Done developed to achieve the Nexus Sprint Goal at the Nexus Sprint Review in order to receive stakeholder feedback.

Nexus Daily Scrum

The Nexus Daily Scrum is an event for appropriate representatives from individual Development Teams to inspect the current state of the Integrated Increment and to identify integration issues or newly discovered cross-team dependencies or cross-team impacts.

During the Nexus Daily Scrum, attendees should focus on each team's impact on the Integrated Increment and discuss:

1. Was the previous day's work successfully integrated? If not, why not?

2. What new dependencies or impacts have been identified?

3. What information needs to be shared across teams in the Nexus?

The Development Teams uses the Nexus Daily Scrum to inspect progress toward the Nexus Sprint Goal. At least every Nexus Daily Scrum, the Nexus Sprint Backlog should be adjusted to reflect the current understanding of the work of the Scrum Teams within the Nexus.

The individual Scrum Teams then take back issues and work that were identified during the Nexus Daily Scrum to their individual Scrum Teams for planning inside their individual Daily Scrum events.

Nexus Sprint Review

The Nexus Sprint Review is held at the end of the Sprint to provide feedback on the Integrated Increment that the Nexus has built over the Sprint and to adapt the Product Backlog if needed.

A Nexus Sprint Review replaces individual Scrum Team Sprint Reviews, because the entire Integrated Increment is the focus for capturing feedback from stakeholders. It may not be possible to show all completed work in detail. Techniques may be necessary to maximize stakeholder feedback. The result of the Nexus Sprint Review is a revised Product Backlog.

Nexus Sprint Retrospective

The Nexus Sprint Retrospective is a formal opportunity for a Nexus to inspect and adapt itself and create a plan for improvements to be enacted during the next Sprint to ensure continuous improvement. The Nexus Sprint Retrospective occurs after the Nexus Sprint Review and prior to the next Nexus Sprint Planning.

It consists of three parts:

1. The first part is an opportunity for appropriate representatives from across a Nexus to meet and identify issues that have impacted more than a single team. The purpose is to make shared issues transparent to all Scrum Teams.

2. The second part consists of each Scrum Team holding their own Sprint Retrospective as described in the Scrum framework. They can use issues raised from the first part of the Nexus Retrospective as input to their team discussions. The individual Scrum Teams should form actions to address these issues during their individual Scrum Team Sprint Retrospectives.

3. The final, third part is an opportunity for appropriate representatives from the Scrum Teams to meet again and agree on how to visualize and track the identified actions. This allows the Nexus as a whole to adapt.

Because they are common scaling dysfunctions, every Retrospective should address the following subjects:

*   Was any work left undone? Did the Nexus generate technical debt?

- Were all artifacts, particularly code, frequently (as often as every day) successfully integrated?

- Was the software successfully built, tested, and deployed often enough to prevent the overwhelming accumulation of unresolved dependencies?

For the questions above, address if necessary:

- Why did this happen?

- How can technical debt be undone?

- How can the recurrence be prevented?

Nexus Artifacts

Artifacts represent work or value to provide transparency and opportunities for inspection and adaptation, as described in the Scrum Guide.

Product Backlog

There is a single Product Backlog for the entire Nexus and all of its Scrum Teams. The Product Owner is accountable for the Product Backlog, including its content, availability, and ordering.

At scale, the Product Backlog must be understood at a level where dependencies can be detected and minimized. To support resolution, Product Backlog Items are often resolved to a granularity called "thinly sliced" functionality. Product Backlog Items are deemed "Ready" for the Nexus Sprint Planning meeting when the Scrum Teams can select items to be done with no or minimal dependencies with other Scrum Teams.

Nexus Sprint Backlog

A Nexus Sprint Backlog is the composite of Product Backlog Items from the Sprint Backlogs of the individual Scrum Teams. It is used to highlight dependencies and the flow of work during the Sprint. It is updated at least daily, often as part of the Nexus Daily Scrum.

Integrated Increment

The Integrated Increment represents the current sum of all integrated work completed by a Nexus. The Integrated Increment must be usable and potentially releasable which means it must meet the Definition of Done. The Integrated Increment is inspected at the Nexus Sprint Review.

Artifact Transparency

Just like its building block, Scrum, Nexus is based on transparency. The Nexus Integration Team works with the Scrum Teams within a Nexus and the organization to ensure that transparency is apparent across all artifacts and that the integrated state of the Integrated Increment is widely understood.

Decisions made based on the state of Nexus artifacts are only as effective as the level of artifact transparency. Incomplete or partial information will lead to incorrect or flawed decisions. The impact of those decisions can be magnified at the scale of Nexus. Software must be developed so that dependencies are detected and resolved before technical debt becomes unacceptable to the Nexus. A lack of complete transparency will make it impossible to guide a Nexus effectively to minimize risk and maximize value.

Definition of Done

The Nexus Integration Team is responsible for a Definition of Done that can be applied to the Integrated Increment developed each Sprint. All Scrum Teams of a Nexus adhere to this Definition of Done. The Increment is Done only when integrated, usable and potentially releasable by the Product Owner.

Individual Scrum Teams may choose to apply a more stringent Definition of Done within their own teams, but cannot apply less rigorous criteria than agreed for the Increment.

Sprint Length for Multiple Scrum Teams

The Scrum framework does not require the same Sprint length or aligned Sprints for all teams.

However, if several teams work together using the Nexus Framework, they work in the same Nexus Sprint, have common Nexus Sprint Planning and other events. The teams should use (but it is not must) the same Sprint length and all Sprints should start and finish together to avoid inefficiency. Another option could be when one team has 2 week Sprint length, whereas another teams use 4 weeks. Usually there are many ways to solve the inefficiencies. However, definitely not by making something prescriptive.

Multiple Scrum Teams working on the same Product may or may not have the same Sprint start date.

Sample Questions

Q: In Matha Globals, Agile Scrum was adopted and management wanted to scale it to larger teams. They know a scaled Scrum has more than one Scrum Team working from the same Product Backlog, but they were discussing on whether to go with one Product Owner for all Scrum Team or one Product Owner for each Scrum Team. Four Scrum teams were formed, working on one product with a single Product Backlog and one Product Owner. Six Sprints with two weeks duration each completed successfully. Management wants to improve the productivity of the teams; hence, they decided to compare the performance of each Development Team. They wanted to standardize velocity across all four teams. Help yourself in selecting true statements from following. Select all applicable

1. Velocity has no direct relationship with value.
2. Velocity is a measure of the value a team produces. The sum of the sizes of all the completed Product Backlog Items in a Sprint is the team's velocity for that Sprint
3. The Development Team uses the Daily Scrum to inspect progress toward the Sprint Goal, to calculate velocity in Daily Scrum and to inspect how progress is trending toward completing the work in the Sprint Backlog
4. Implementing a PBI of size 20 does not mean it will deliver more value than completing a PBI of size 15

Q: Kane a senior developer is eager to know more on scaling Scrum as product demand is increased and a lot of new features needs to be developed. Two Scrum Teams were added and all were working on the same product. Kane said, in Scaled Scrum, every Development Team should show its specific Increment in a separate branch of the code to ease interdependence between Development Teams and each team provides a separate Increment with the functionality developed by the individual team. Do you agree with Kane? True or False

Q: Jeanne the Scrum Master, Emma the Product Owner and four Scrum teams are developing a product together. Sprint duration is 2 weeks. Three Sprints are completed and integrated Product Increment is very accepted in the market. Which of the following statements is true.

1. The Product Owner is responsible for maximizing the value of the product resulting from the work of the Development Team.

2. As the breathing period is required in the first Sprint, integration is less critical in the first Sprint and can be skipped for the first Sprint only. It is still possible to release functionality that is not integrated and has the potential business value at the decision of the Product Owner.

3. The Scrum Master is responsible for maximizing the value of the product.

4. The Scrum Team is responsible for maximizing the value of the product

Q: A new developer Neil has just joined one Development Team which were following scaled Scrum. Neil asked Scrum Master Adam about significance of the Sprint Review meeting in scaled Scrum. Adam said, in Sprint Review, each team provides a separate Increment with the functionality developed by the individual team. The Sprint Review meeting is used to identify the work needed to integrate with the other teams. This work is then added to the Product Backlog. Do you agree with Adam? Yes or No.

Q: Usually there is only one Product Owner for product development. When the product to be developed is too complicated, there could be two Product Owners (Primary and Backup). True or False

Q: A Developer Carl was working simultaneously on multiple Scrum teams. He feels is less productive than a person working on a single Scrum Team. Do you agree with Carl? True or False

Q: In scaled Scrum, multiple teams working on the same product can have the same Sprint Backlog. True or False

Q: In Maheshvara Global Software organization, four Scrum teams are working on a product development. Abraham is a subject matter expert (on Adaptive AUTOSAR technology) for these four Scrum teams, and Beyonce is the Scrum Master. Several developers ask Beyonce that Akraham is needed full-time for the work identified for the next four Sprints as all new features are based on AUTOSAR. What do you think Beyonce can do in this situation?

1. Beyonce can allot Akraham to one team per Sprint, over the four Sprints each team can have the support it needs.

2. Beyonce can ask Akraham to work overtime (2 hours per day) as it is only needed for the next four Sprints and then he can go on long vacations.

3. Beyonce can inform Development Team that SMEs are always busy and cannot be allocated full time for them. They will have to learn the new technology on their own.

4. Beyonce can ask Development Team in what manner they need to handle this problem and facilitate them to implement their chosen solution.

5. Beyonce can ask Product Owner to provide the solution as ultimately the Product Owner is accountable for the product.

Q: Oprah is a senior developer working with Nirguna Software. In her organization many teams wants to adopt scaled Scrum. However, they are not sure when multiple Scrum teams are working on the same product, how should requirements be distributed among the multiple Development Teams. Help yourself in selecting the true statements from the following. Select all applicable

1. They must be selected from one Product Backlog in such a way that each Scrum Team has an equal volume of requirements per Sprint.

2. The Scrum team, with the highest velocity should get the preference and allow them to first pull the Product Backlog Items from the Product Backlog.

3. All developers are not equal in skills and competencies. Highly competent Development Team should get complex requirements for implementation and low priority requirements should be kept for less experiences Development Team.

4. Ultimately, the Product Owner is accountable for the product. To avoid complexity and conflicts among Development Teams, the Product Owner can provide separate Product Backlog to each Development Team.

5. None of the above

Q: In a multi-national organization, for building one new product, four new Scrum teams are formed. As Scrum was new in the organization, many associates have lot of questions on Scrum framework. Scrum trainings were arranged while working on actual product development. Few developers asked Scrum Master Marilyn who will coordinate the effort between the different Scrum Teams working on this same product. What do you think, Marilyn should do? Select all applicable

1. Coach the Development Teams to work in separate branches and create a separate integration Sprint after every two-development Sprints. Senior developers can coordinate for the integration Sprint.

2. Marilyn should visit the four Development Teams each day to coordinate their work so that Development Teams can focus on the development work and not on how to coordinate.

3. Marilyn should ask the Development Teams to update the task board daily in Daily Scrum and inform her each day.

4. Teach Development Teams that it is their responsibility to form teams of developers with the skills to create an integrated Increment every Sprint.

3. Adoption of Agile in an Organization

Taking the first step in moving to Agile in an organizational can be challenging because of the organization culture (challenge in shifting the mindset of the people involved) and general resistance to change. Adoption become more challenging if you need to get your customers to adapt Agile, as customers may also resist to change.

What needs to be in place (or well thought out) even before you start making changes to your organization? Answer is – correct environment.

- Assess readiness of organizations – Organizations should assess their readiness and prepare for the change needed for Agile by developing a roadmap to get to an Agile development environment.

- Start small and not attempt all projects in the entire organization in one go – You need to start small and implement Agile within one or two teams initially. Once these teams can handle everything on their own, move towards the next teams.

- Right infrastructure – You need to provide workspace (space-efficient, productive, and vibrant) that will ease the communication and team members' interaction.

- Right Training – Training plans needs to be developed for everyone to develop new skills and new ways of thinking. Everyone should complete the trainings, self-learning courses and self-evaluations. Associates should start practicing Agile practices (Ex. Time-boxing) and practice of creating Agile artifacts (Ex. Writing User Stories).

- Communicate to customers – You should explain to customer why you are shifting to Agile and what they can expect from you. By engaging the customer the right way, they will become more comfortable and excited to work in a collaborative way.

- Executives, managers and leaders should let go the temptation to micro-manage. With proper Agile coaching, leaders can learn how to develop collaborative relationship with team and empower team members to make decisions.

- Lack of experience – If the organization does not have Agile experienced associates (Scrum Master, Product Owner) then the HR department should know the characteristics of a good Scrum Master or Product Owner, in order to hire someone for the job.

- Modern communication technologies – People involved should be able to connect to each other whenever they need, especially for distributed teams (different office and different time zones). Organization should provide collaboration tools (Skype, Google Hangouts, video conference, screen share, headsets, audio conference, Jira, Confluence ,etc.).

- Pull changes – How teams adopting Agile is more important than someone asking them to follow Agile practices. If teams start recognizing that a problem exists in current approach (before adopting the Agile) then they will pull (instead of push) changes needed for adopting Agile.

- Onsite Offshore project execution – Team should develop product ownership, develop project domain experts, experts in project work area at different locations (onsite, offshore). This will reduce dependency across locations especially due to time zone. Team should simulate the test environment, test data and use the continuous integration tools (Jenkins, Perforce, etc.).

4. Agile is a Transformational Journey

I want to start with a very good poem.

Life is too short,
grudges are a waste of perfect happiness.

Laugh when you can,
apologize when you should
and let go of what you can't change.

Love deeply and forgive quickly.
Take chances, give everything
and have no regrets.

Life is too short to be unhappy.
You have to take the good with the bad,
smile when you're sad,
love what you got
and always remember what you had.

Always forgive but never forget.
Learn from your mistakes
but never regret.

People change,
and things go wrong
but always remember...
LIFE GOES ON !!!

Whenever conflict occurs while working with others, which is beyond your control. Look again at this poem's words they give good advice; it makes a lot of sense.

I am writing this story in the context of a realistic but fictional organization. This allows readers to learn more effectively by losing themselves in a story and by being able to relate to the characters. I hope it helps your team overcome its fear of Agile transformation so that it can achieve more than individuals could ever imagine doing alone.

People were in constant pain, releasing the deliverables in every 4–5 months, for some projects it was 6–8 months, and for few projects towards the end of project. People were working on weekends, late nights. Where team ended up is much happier place and people were smiling. At the end of transformation, team's quality was amazing. People life changed dramatically.

One day everyone in the organization got mail, decision taken was to be Agile in next two years. Right decision taken by CEO of ArundhatiSoft, Pune based capable company of the Indian IT sector.

Organization started working on providing the right infrastructure (workspace, communication channels) and Agile trainings. Agile COE group was formed.

Team:

✓ Alexander – Program Manager, IT Department

Alexander had managed several end-to-end deliveries from project initiation to project closure. He had managed business operations like billing to client, allocation/de allocation of resources and onsite/offshore management.

He is managing 10+ project teams, each team is having 4–8 team members. He is handling around 70 team members. Each team is working on different project for different client managers of WashLeBright, Inc, Russia.

✓ Amreen, Donna, Jennifer, Anushka – Project Leads, IT Department

They all are leading 2–3 teams each. All are following standards and processes set by the organization for software development projects.

✓ Sunny – Project Leader, IT Department

Sunny is leading seven offshore team members working from Pune, India. He was never rude and a very people friendly leader. Project was going on from last six months. Sunny had to spend a lot of time in negotiating with his client Anna.

✓ Eric – Onsite coordinator, IT Department

Eric is working at client location as an onsite coordinator. He has good knowledge of product domain and client has appreciated his work many times.

✓ Anna – Product Manager, WashLeBright, Russia

Experienced in planning and developing the software products for WashLeBright. Demanding and always asks software Development Team to use latest architecture, new technology and framework. Changes the requirements as per market demand.

Transformation started

Alexander has asked his Learning Management department to arrange Scrum training session focused for his teams. All have attended with great excitement. They have learned a lot in two days Scrum session. Few team members were discussing to implement Scum in their projects.

Days, weeks, months passed but no one had implemented Scrum and teams were busy in daily project work. Changing the mindset of the people is not easy, especially when they have worked in a particular way for several years. There was a resistance to change.

Alexander has observed that there were approximately 20–25 % early adopters, those who supported for change by motivating by something new. 50% were ready to follow standards and guidelines. Remaining 25% were not willing to change unless management were telling them to change.

One day Sunny came to Alexander and informed him that client Anna was not happy with the project deliverables. Anna was saying team had not understood the requirement and product was not built as per her expectations. She wanted team to implement the requirements without extending the delivery date and without any additional cost. Sunny informed Alexander that team is capable and doing their best. Many times associates are working overtime and are coming to office on weekends to work on changes in requirements from Anna. Team was working very hard, however could not receive positive feedback from the client. Product was getting failed and people got disappointed. Associates were getting demotivated and attrition rate started increasing within the project/group. Associates did not thought of – "Life is too short to be unhappy. You have to take the good with the bad"...

Sunny was thinking on something for a while and then said I wish my team and I should have started following the Scrum. Alexander asked Sunny why we could not start adopting Agile right now. Sunny said, he will discuss with his team and with client Anna and will start adopting Agile Scrum positively. This is what – "and always remember what you had."

Alexander was aware of benefits of Agile. He started creating an environment of engagement with his teams for adopting Agile in his group. Started discussing with teams in-person on weekly basis on Agile adoption. Alexander hired one Agile coach, Marie.

After couple of weeks, post discussion with associates, few teams decided to adopt at least couple of Scrum practices across few projects. Daily Scrum was started. Teams started discussing with their clients to reduce the delivery cycles to 2–4 weeks instead of 3–4 months (or even more than that). Teams created a list of things the team want to stop doing and teams also created a list of the things they want to start doing. With the help from Marie, team had started adopting Scrum meetings.

Teams started using modern collaboration tools like Skype, Google Hangouts, video conference, screen share, headsets, audio conference, Digital whiteboard, and Team Foundation Server (TFS). Telephone & network was distributed throughout. Few teams were using task board (Physical or Digital) to visualize the progress and improve team transparency. What the team did is – Take chances, give everything and have no regrets.

Sunny completed the Professional Scrum Master (PSM I) Certification. With Agile coaching from Marie, Sunny learned how to develop collaborative relationship with team and empower team members to make decisions. Sunny was not sure whether he should be the Scrum Master for his team. He read somewhere that project leads should not become Scrum Master in Agile projects as leads may start their traditional monitoring and controlling conducts. However, he was very eager to become Scrum Master and adopt Scrum by heart. He discussed with Marie and Alexander and they decided to give him this opportunity.

Sunny and Development Team discussed with Anna, they explained to Anna why they want to shift to Agile and she understood the benefits of Agile. She was very happy to know that team has found a solution for delivering product with the improved quality. Anna also took training on Scrum and understood the role of Product Owner. Scrum Team (Anna, Sunny, and Development Team) agreed for two weeks Sprint and delivering potentially shippable Product Increment in each Sprint.

Scrum Team was performing Sprint Planning meeting with a time box of 4 hours. Team was planning their work to be performed in the Sprint in this meeting. They were discussing with Anna on the most important Product Backlog Items to build in the Sprint. Scrum Team was crafting a Sprint Goal that was specific and measurable. Sprint Goal was guiding the Development Team on why they are building the Product Increment. Development Team was creating

Sprint Backlog by pulling the work based on average work completed in previous Sprints and no one was pushing them to work on any particular activity.

Development Team was doing Daily Scrum at 10 a.m. for 15 minutes in conference room number 3. Initially, Sunny facilitated Daily Scrum meetings and helped Development Team to complete Daily Scrum in time-box of 15 minutes. Once team was capable enough to manage the Daily Scum on their own; Sunny was not attending the Daily Scrum. Development Team was ensuring a focused Daily Scrum as they using Sprint Goal to inspect their progress.

Few associates who felt like nothing will ever change, after first delivery, they get their hopes up and after second delivery, they believed in themselves. Team members started responding and getting motivated. Earlier there was resistance but after initial progressive delivers, it was much easier. Team was collaborating and was becoming more and more self-organized. Six Sprints completed successfully. "Learn from your mistakes but never regret."

Development Team had developed a checklist (Definition of Done) of the types of work that the team was expected to complete and were updating Definition of Done as and when needed. Team was using the Customer Satisfaction, Employee Satisfaction, Burndown Chart, and Capacity chart as Key Value Measures.

One of the developer, Robert started coming late to Daily Scum meeting by 5–6 minutes. All developers had to wait for him in the meeting and hence could not finish the Daily Scrum by 10:15 a.m. Sunny was observing this, however, he decided not to give solution to team and let Development Team resolve this issue on their own. After couple of days, developers as a self-organizing team decided to change the Daily Scrum timing to 11 a.m. so that everyone can reach on time. Sunny was happy to see Development Team resolved this issue themselves.

Team was enjoying Agile way of working. The progress of development was visible, Scrum team was able to adapt to changing requirements. Anna was also engaging with team. Anna was writing project requirements in User Story format in Product Backlog. She has asked Eric to help her in writing the User Stories. Sometimes she used to delegate this activity to Eric. Anna was considering Eric as Clone Product Owner (Note – there is no term called as Clone or Proxy Product Owner in Scrum Guide). Anna has given some authority to Eric so that Eric can take decisions in case she is not available due to any unavoidable reasons.

One day, developer Rosa has informed team about her marriage plan in next month and after marriage, she would be shifting to some other city where ArundhatiSoft does not have any branch. Justin joined their team as a replacement for Rosa. Justin was a known important figure in ArundhatiSoft, many senior managers and executives knows him very well.

Justin was very talkative and many developers found his discussions interesting. During the Daily Scrum, Justin speaks a lot that takes up all the time in the Daily Scrum and developers are not able to complete Daily Scrum in 15 minutes. Sunny was observing and he did not do anything, as self-organizing Development Team needs to resolve their problems. As Justin was a known figure, team was hesitant to tell him the reason behind this problem. After few more days, developers decided to start passing a token around system during Daily Scrum, where the developer holding the token would be the only one allowed to speak. They tried this but did not worked well, as many times it becomes necessity that other developers provides their suggestions. Sunny understood that issue was becoming the obstacle and further delay would impact the project; Sunny did the coaching to Justin and helped him to understand the impact on Daily Scrum. Justin thanked Sunny for coaching him and Daily Scrum meeting was completing in time-box of 15 minutes.

Scrum Team was performing Sprint Review meeting with a time-box of 2 hours. Anna was usually participating with her end users and business team. One of the developer on rotation basis was leading this meeting and was demonstrating the work done to all present in the meeting. Anna and all participants were giving early feedback and product quality was improving. Early delivery of business value in each Sprint lowered the risk associated with development.

Scrum Team was performing Sprint Retrospective meeting with a time-box of 1.5 hours. Team was identifying ways to increase product quality by improving work processes. Sunny was encouraging the Scrum Team to improve, within the Scrum process framework, its development process, and practices to make it more effective and enjoyable for the next Sprint. "Laugh when you can, apologize when you should..."

Anna was satisfied with the project outcome and also employee satisfaction was visible in the Scrum Team. Scrum team was handling everything on their own. Alexander's few more teams adopted Agile.

In ArundhatiSoft, organization culture was changed, employees' life was changing, behavior was changing, and expectation and goal was changing. Now, Alexander's all teams are 100% Agile.

That's why I believe in – "People change, and things go wrong but always remember...LIFE GOES ON !!!"

References

- Adkins, Lyssa. 2010. *Coaching Agile Teams. A Companion for Scrum Masters, Agile Coaches, and Project Managers in Transition.*

- Agile Alliance. *https://www.agilealliance.org/agile101/.*

- American Society for Quality. https://asq.org/quality-resources/lean/value-stream-mapping.

- Basha, Akbar. 2019. Scrum at life. *https://www.linkedin.com/pulse/values-Scrum-akbar-basha-md.*

- Beck, Kent, Mike Beedle, Arie van Bennekum, Alistair Cockburn, Ward Cunningham, Martin Fowler, James Grenning, Jim Highsmith, Andrew Hunt, Ron Jeffries, Jon Kern, Brian Marick, Robert C. Martin, Steve Mellor, Ken Schwaber, Jeff Sutherland, Dave Thomas. 2001. *Manifesto for Agile Software Development. https://agilemanifesto.org/.*

- Casanova, Jose. November 7, 2017. *http://www.joseacasanova.com/2017/11/07/how-being-a-facilitator-makes-you-an-elite-Scrum-master/*

- Cohn, Mike. 2004. *User Stories Applied: For Agile Software Development.*

- Cohn, Mike. 2006. *Agile Estimating and Planning.*

- Cohn, Mike. 2009. *Succeeding with Agile.*

- Fridman, Adam. *https://www.inc.com/adam-fridman/the-massive-downside-of-agile-software-development.html.*

- Laing Samantha and Karen Greaves. 2015. *Growing Agile. A Coach's Guide to Agile Testing.*

- Gunther, Verheyen. 2019. *Scrum a Pocket Guide.*

- Gunther, Verheyen. *https://guntherverheyen.com*

- Howard, Eric. September 5, 2018. *https://www.simio.com/blog/2018/09/05/evolution-industrial-ages-industry-1–0-4–0/.*

- InfoQ.com. *https://www.infoq.com/articles/sutherland-Scrum/.*

- Jeff Sutherland. *Scrum – The art of doing twice the work in half the time.*

- Juliana Willsey. September 4,1992. *https://www.poemhunter.com/poem/life-is-too-short-9/*

- Ken Schwaber and Mike Beedle. 2002. *Agile Software Development with Scrum.*

- Kendis Team. October 16, 2018. *https://kendis.io/scaling-agile/comparison-agile-scaling-models/.*

- Lapshin, Mikhail. 2019. *https://mlapshin.com/index.php/blog/Scrum-questions/.*

- Miro. *https://miro.com/blog/choose-between-agile-lean-Scrum-kanban/.*

- Nagarajah, Sasha. *https://www.globalapptesting.com/blog/is-software-development-like-manufacturing.*

- Oliver, Scott. *https://medium.com/serious-scrum/10-tips-to-improve-your-daily-scrum-f3d66946a487.*

- Overeem, Barry. April 15, 2016. *https://www.infoq.com/articles/great-scrum-team/*

- Pichler, Roman. March 11, 2014. *https://www.romanpichler.com/blog/Sprint-goal-template/.*

- PlanView LeanKit. *https://leankit.com/learn/lean/lean-and-agile-development/*.

- Stackify. *https://stackify.com/continuous-delivery-vs-continuous-deployment-vs-continuous-integration/*.

- Schwaber, Ken and Jeff Sutherland. November 2017. *The Scrum Guide. www.scrumguides.org.*

- Schwaber, Ken and Scrum.Org. January 2018. *Nexus Guide – The Definitive Guide to scaling Scrum with Nexus: The Rules of the Game.*

- Scrum.org. 2019. *www.Scrum.org/Resources.*

- Scrum.org. 2019. *www.Scrum.org/Community.*

- Scrum.org and Daniel Vacant. April 2018. *The Kanban Guide for Scrum Teams.*

- Scrum.org. *Evidence-Based Management Guide. January 2019.*

- SlideShare. *https://www.slideshare.net/wso2.org/transport-for-londons-transition-to-agile-delivery.*

- Roman Pichler. February 8, 2010. *https://www.romanpichler.com/blog/make-the-product-backlog-deep/*.

- Rubin, Kenneth. 2015. *Essential Scrum. A practical guide to the most popular Agile process.*

- Takeuchi, Hirotaka and Nonaka, Ikujiro. January 1, 1986. *https://hbsp.harvard.edu/product/86116-PDF-ENG*

- Theintactone.com. *https://theintactone.com/2019/02/19/ism-u3-topic-6-Waterfall-method/*

- The Scrum Master.co.uk. *https://www.thescrummaster.co.uk/Scrum/the-five-Scrum-events/*

- Trapps, Steve. March 14, 2018. *https://www.Scrum.org/resources/blog/visualising-Scrum-values*

- Tudor, D. 17 January 2013. *https://www.certifytoinspire.com/wp-content/uploads/2013/01/Sample-Questions-with-Answers-for-Web-Revised-Jan-2013-v0–3.pdf.*

- Vara, Jiten. August 14, 2014. *https://scrumandkanban.co.uk/coaching-v-mentoring/.*

- Virtualprojectoffice. September 22, 2017. *https://virtualprojectoffice.wordpress.com/2017/09/22/pms-corner-disadvantages-of-agile/.*

- Wake, Bill. August 17, 2003. *https://xp123.com/articles/invest-in-good-stories-and-smart-tasks/*

www.ingramcontent.com/pod-product-compliance
Lightning Source LLC
Chambersburg PA
CBHW051045050326
40690CB00006B/605